About the author

Samantha Hahn is an author and actress, most recently having made her Off-Broadway debut as Beylke in *Fiddler on the Roof in Yiddish*. She studies musical theatre at Manhattan School of Music, and is the voice of Trinket the Unicorn on Nick Jr.'s *Nella The Princess Knight* in both the US and UK. Samantha is currently storytelling in New York City. Official website: sammyhahn.com

ON THE ROOF
A LOOK INSIDE *FIDDLER ON THE ROOF* IN
YIDDISH

SAMANTHA HAHN

ON THE ROOF
A LOOK INSIDE *FIDDLER ON THE ROOF IN YIDDISH*

Vanguard Press

VANGUARD PAPERBACK

© Copyright 2020
Samantha Hahn

The right of Samantha Hahn to be identified as author of
this work has been asserted by her in accordance with the
Copyright, Designs and Patents Act 1988.

A CIP catalogue record for this title is
available from the British Library.

ISBN 9781784658649

*Vanguard Press is an imprint of
Pegasus Elliot MacKenzie Publishers Ltd.*
www.pegasuspublishers.com

First Published in 2020

**Vanguard Press
Sheraton House Castle Park
Cambridge England**

Printed & Bound in Great Britain

Dedication

Dedicated to all of my Mishpokhe.

Acknowledgements

I started this book by dragging my loving castmates into the stairwell at intermission during the show and asking them to talk about their experience. I'm endlessly grateful for everyone who met me in cramped corners backstage or in the theatre to entertain my random questions. Your words are what make this book so beautiful to me. Thank you to my parents, Zalmen Mlotek, Rachel Zatcoff, and Raquel Nobile for your endless and unwavering support on this ambitious project. I love you all. Thank you to Jamibeth Margolis for bringing the Fiddler family together, and to everyone who has ever been involved in this special show. The biggest thank you to Joel Grey for inspiring me, bringing me into this family, and teaching me more than I can say. You are always right. Thank you to everyone at Pegasus for bringing this story to life.

Part One
Chutzpah

Sammy

Role: Beylke

I was nearing the end of my sophomore year of college at Manhattan School of Music, and coming up on the tech week for our production of the musical *Smile*, when I saw an audition post for *Fiddler on the Roof in Yiddish*. The post said that they were looking for a male or female violinist who is also a strong actor/mover: a type that I by no means identified with. I loved *Fiddler on the Roof*, though, and I wanted to audition for it. I emailed the casting director, Jamibeth Margolis, and said, "I can't play the violin but I can sing, act, and move and would love to be considered for a role in *Fiddler on the Roof in Yiddish*." Much to my excitement, I received an email back the next day with an appointment and audition sides for Beylke and Shprintze, Tevye's two youngest daughters. I went to the head of my program and told him about the audition, and he said I was not allowed to go because I would be missing part of a tech rehearsal for *Smile*. I had never missed a rehearsal before, so I made the gutsy decision to interpret his disapproval as a mere personal piece of advice. I quickly emailed the stage manager and directors of *Smile* at my school and said, "I have an audition for a project that is very important to me, and I need to be late to this tech rehearsal. I can't miss the audition, but I will be as quick as possible getting back. Thank you so much in advance for understanding." My stage manager emailed me back and said, "Be as fast as you can, and break a leg at your audition."

On April 19th, 2018, I ran around the dorms in search of a long skirt to borrow, printed off all the sides, and started working on the Yiddish with the little pronunciation recordings that were attached to the audition email. Motl Didner, the associate director and Yiddish coach, had recorded tracks of himself reading the Yiddish sides for us, which was very helpful to me since I had not heard much of the language before. I practiced until I had everything memorized and was comfortable enough with the material that I could work on making acting choices and having fun with it. I called my mom and sang "Matchmaker" in Yiddish for her because I knew that she would love to hear it. I watched the *Fiddler on the Roof* movie and pictured myself as one of the little girls who jumped in front of the window at the end of the "Matchmaker" scene. On the day of the audition, I hopped on the one train after class with a heavy backpack and a change of clothes for tech rehearsal. I was practicing my lines on the way there and singing "Matchmaker" out loud on the subway like a crazy person, when I realized that I had forgotten to look up how to pronounce the names of the characters I was auditioning for. They didn't include the names of the characters in the recording we were sent, and I had absolutely no idea how to pronounce "Beylke" or "Shprintze." I frantically searched on Google, but the service on the train was terrible and I couldn't find anything helpful. I kept practicing the sides and just prayed that nobody would ask me which characters I was auditioning for. To my relief, no one ever asked me. I got to the audition, signed in, and waited to be sent in the room. When I walked in, there was a panel of people — with Joel Grey sitting right in the middle. I looked at everyone and smiled, introduced myself, and before I knew it, I was singing "Matchmaker" in Yiddish. When I was finished singing, Joel Grey looked at me and said, "That was just so sweet. How about the sides?" I read the sides with Motl Didner, and Joel said, "Perfect." Then Motl said, "Can you try that last line again, and really roll the "r" there?" I thought, *oh man, I totally can't roll my "r's. This is going to be awkward.* I tried and failed to roll the "r" and thought, *well, at least I had fun.* They said, "Thank you," and I said, "Thanks! Nice to see you all," and walked out of the room. Then I ran outside, changed my clothes, hopped on the one train back to school, and ran in late to my tech rehearsal. I checked in with the assistant stage manager, then threw on my mic and some rehearsal clothes and slipped onto the stage like I had been there the whole time. The next morning, I got a really bad cold.

A few days later I got an email that said I had a callback for Shprintze and Beylke. I was pretty overjoyed. They had given me a tricky new page of Yiddish to learn and asked me to prepare that along with the original material. I practiced everything again and got to play around with some more choices, but I was recovering from my cold and my voice was a little shaky. The callback was in about three days so I just hoped that I would recover by then; I was steaming and doing all of the remedies I could think of. We had our Sitzprobe for *Smile* at school that night and our music director already knew that I was going to be marking everything because I wasn't feeling well. After the first song at the Sitzprobe, I realized I could barely sing at all so I stopped singing with the ensemble numbers. I tried to do a couple of my solo lines, but they barely came out of me. I caught eyes with my music director, and he told me to sit this one out because I clearly couldn't sing. I went on complete vocal rest for the night, steamed before bed, and when I woke up my voice was still gone. I could barely speak, so I was freaking out. I had all of this new Yiddish material to learn and I had no voice to practice it with. I kept my mouth shut all day, tried to learn the Yiddish in my head by listening to the recording, and prayed that I would wake up with a voice for the callback the next day. When I woke up the next morning, I chugged two glasses of water, showered, steamed, and then tried to do a vocal trill. I pretty much jumped up and down with relief and joy when a sound came out of me. I did maybe three little vocal warm-ups and everything seemed good, so I ran my sides and the song out loud once. Then I shut my mouth again and went down to the callbacks, praying that my voice would last.

At the callbacks there were a bunch of girls dressed exactly like me who were auditioning for Shprintze and Beylke. They called us all into a room and the choreographer, Staś Kmieć, taught us the daughters' dance in "Tradition." The same panel of the creative and casting team from the audition was watching us; the room had a very friendly feel to it, so even though it was nerve wracking, I was having a lot of fun. We did a final round of the dance so the creative team and casting could watch, and then Joel called us over to the audition table. He told us to go down the line and say our names, ages, and a little bit about ourselves. I said, "Hi, I'm Samantha, I'm twenty years old, I have two older sisters, I go to Manhattan School of Music… and, yeah, it's really fun!" Then this girl that I didn't know, who was on the other end of the line leaned out and said, "Oh my gosh, you go to Manhattan School of Music? I went there!"

I said, "No way! That's so cool," and we had a fun little moment. That girl was Raquel Nobile, who ended up being the Shprintze to my Beylke and is one of my very best friends.

I went back to school after that and finished off my

day, having had so much fun at the audition and feeling happy that my voice was back. After class I went to our *Smile* dress rehearsal and everyone was pleased that I could finally speak and sing again. Soon it was our opening night and I wasn't thinking about the callback at all. I usually try to leave everything in the audition room no matter what the project, and this seemed like such an amazing long shot that I truly wasn't thinking about anything coming from it. We had our opening night of *Smile* and my whole family was there: my mom, dad, sisters, and my Mom-Mom. When my family was walking me back to the dorms after the show, my Mom-Mom said, "I heard you've been singing "Matchmaker" in Yiddish! I would just love to hear that." I said something along the lines of, "What, doing a whole show for you wasn't enough?" Of course I then sang it to her on the walk back, which made her so happy. My family all left, and I got ready for bed, really thinking about the callback for the first time and how I wished I had gotten it. I was under the covers with the lights off, in the midst of setting my phone to silent when I got an email with subject line: "Offer for *Fiddler on the Roof*". I immediately started crying. I jumped out of bed and just started running down the hallway of the dorms. I tried to call every member of my family and none of them would pick up the phone, so I started texting my friends in the dorms to see who was awake. Everyone was sleeping, except for my friends Liam and Jo who were right down the hall from me. I ran into their room and told them what happened, and we all jumped up and down together while I started crying even more. They were so excited for me, and we read the email together and talked about how amazing it was going to be. We toasted to my Off-Broadway debut with liquid Nyquil shots, because it was time to go to sleep. Just as I was getting in bed, my mom called me back; apparently my whole family had been charging their phones and that's why they couldn't pick up. I told them that I got the offer to play Beylke in *Fiddler*; they all cheered excitedly for me, and then I went to sleep. I went to class the next day, and the day after that, until I finished out my year as a sophomore — quietly knowing that I would be making my Off-Broadway debut that summer in *Fiddler on the Roof in Yiddish.*

* * *

Raquel Nobile

Role: Shprintze | Hodl Understudy

Initially they told us: "Good news! Shprintze and Beylke get to be in Matchmaker, Chavalah Ballet, and Anatevka!" We were so excited. I thought, *Yes! This is so cool; I get to be in pretty much the whole show.* On the first day of rehearsal we started singing in the end of "Matchmaker," doing the harmonies and everything. A couple of days later we went to choreograph the number.

Staś, our choreographer, gave us each a broom, and said, "This is going to be the suitor." So Sammy Hahn, who plays Beylke, is holding one broom and I'm holding another, and we're on opposite ends of the stage. We walk on like we're about to be sweeping something, and then the brooms are taken from us and used to demonstrate the suitors that Tsaytl is talking about. The whole thing felt really awkward, and it wasn't long before the brooms got cut. After the brooms were cut, it wasn't long before the two of us got cut from the number entirely. We actually found out about being cut when the older daughters went to a "Matchmaker" rehearsal without us. Then Staś broke the news to us. Pretty soon after that rehearsal, we got brought back. And then we got cut again. It was back and forth for about a week. I think we got cut from "Matchmaker" maybe five times. There were basically two versions of the number that we kept doing for Joel: one with Shprintze and Beylke, and one without. During tech week we had to look at the callboard every day and find out which version we were doing. We ended up being in it almost every day though, and we've been in it ever since. It's evolved a lot from that. At one point we were folding a ton of laundry; now there's a bit with Beylke's glasses.

I remember one day that was really hard for us during all of the changes. That day we got cut from "Matchmaker" again and then on top of that we also got cut from "Anatevka." I just remember looking at Sammy and seeing little tears in her eyes. That's when our stage manager, Kat West, came in and asked what was going on. I said, "It's just kind of been a hard day for the littles." And that's where the term "the littles" got coined. It's what everyone refers to us as now, even when they page us to the wings.

Playing a child is an interesting balance between acting like a kid and finding your inner child. I always have to be sure that I'm not overdoing it or putting on a childlike manner. Instead I try to think of it like this: I try to do each day like I am learning something new. I have all these new experiences, and I just don't hide it on my face. I let it all show. I think I revel in the joyful moments and am confused by the sorrow and sad moments because it's not something that I would have been able to grasp when I was around twelve years old. I really like finding the differences between Shprintze in the first act and Shprintze in the second act. At the start of the show, Shprintze is obviously younger, and she's more innocent, and naive. Then right at the end of the first act the pogrom happens. She doesn't even know what a pogrom is but she suddenly sees the violence, and she fully experiences a pogrom with her family. Then halfway through the second act she comes back on stage, and by this time Motl and Tsaytl have a child so all of this time has gone by for her. She changes her white little bow to a grey headband, and that's what made me start thinking about it — she has seen more, and she's a little bit less energetic and giggly. She loses her three older sisters throughout the show, so that the last scene leaves her as the older sister. She goes from being one of the little carefree ones to being a little bit of a caretaker for Beylke. She is left cheering Beylke up at the end when Beylke is really sad to see Tsaytl leave. They are always the closest two and they are both the little sisters until that moment, when she is left to take care of Beylke. That's what I think about at the end — what our lives will be like in America and what kinds of things I'm going to protect Beylke from, introduce her to, and explore with her.

* * *

Rosie Jo Neddy

Role: Khave

I auditioned for the first time with an excerpt of "Matchmaker" and the scene where Khave tells Tevye she wants to marry Fyedke. In the email it said to cover up and dress a little "shtetl-chic" so I went to Target and bought a long skirt because I owned not one skirt in my entire wardrobe. At the audition table were casting, our choreographer, our music director, and right in the middle was Joel Grey. When I walked in, I had a star-struck moment because I had no idea that Joel would be there for our first audition. I took in Joel and what he looks like now because I'd never seen him in person; all the pictures I've seen of him are from the '70s. I said,

"Hi, how are you?" and everyone at the table said, "Good." Then I looked at them and waited for them to prompt me, expecting them to say, "Why don't we try the scene?" or, "Let's start with the song." They said nothing — it was complete silence. They were all looking at me, so eventually I said, "May we, why don't we start with the song?" They nodded, "Yes."

I went to the pianist and started to give him the music which he obviously already had because everyone was singing "Matchmaker." I got ready to go, and he started the vamp. I've known the song "Matchmaker" since I was about seven years old. I had just learned the Yiddish lyrics so I was crazy nervous about that aspect, but I've always known the melody. I heard the vamp, but I couldn't find my note. I had been singing this song since elementary school. I sang the wrong first couple of notes and immediately said, "Oh my god, can we start again?" We started again and I still couldn't find the note. I ended up having to say, "I'm sorry, can I have my first note?" The pianist finally gave me my first note, and I sang through the song. By that point I was so embarrassed, and I thought that I had blown the audition because it took me three times to start and I head-voiced the high sections. Then they said, "How about the scene?" I was my awkward self and I replied, "Oh yes, the scene… erm-mer-emen-er-mer..." and Joel started to laugh. Then Joel made the noise back at me and asked, "her-mer-ner-men- er?"

I said, "Just, you know, sorting through the files,

hem-in-er-men-er." He laughed more, and then I did the scene. I had it pretty memorized, and at that point I was so emotional from the singing that I was in a good place for the scene. I felt really good about it, and I wasn't watching or judging myself. After I finished the scene, they all said, "Thank you so much" and I started to grab my things because that's usually the cue to leave the audition room. Suddenly Joel said, "Can you sing again?"

I said, "Yes, yes, of course!" I got ready to start to sing again and he said, "But can you sing it like you actually are?"

I said, "Yes." When I sang it that second time, I just tried to be myself and be joyous, and it felt really great. The first time I sang I was trying to act longing and seem more glamorous, but this time I was more grounded and more me. I belted the high note and Joel told me, "Never not sing it like that again." I think Joel gave me a second chance in that moment that I'm very grateful for.

We had a sing-through with the musical director Zalmen before our first official rehearsal. It was to learn the pronunciations and just sing through the show, and it was the first time most of the cast would be at the theatre. I didn't expect anyone to be there except for Zalmen and the cast but Joel was there. That was my first time seeing him out from behind the audition table. He had an armchair on the stage; he was just sitting there. He didn't feel the need to say anything; he wasn't there to interject. He just genuinely wanted to hear the show. We took a break in the middle of the rehearsal, and I ran into Joel on the way to the bathroom. I said, "Hi" and Joel said, "Hi, my dear" and then grabbed hold of both my hands. He started talking to someone else, but he was still holding my hands and then he casually started swaying. Suddenly I was holding hands with Joel Grey and swaying with him. I looked at him and asked, "Are we dancing?" He took a moment and looked back at me and said, "No... but we will someday."

For the first day of rehearsal, I took the six train down to Battery Park, and I took a selfie while walking from the train station to the theatre — trying to look good. They had said in the email there would be pictures taken and to look nice, so I did my makeup and hair and dressed up. I look back on that picture and I look so terrified. I'm smiling, but my eyes are saying I'm about to walk to the guillotine. I walked in and there was a whole step-and-repeat for photos and about twenty different people from the press. There were bagels and I thought, *should I eat a bagel?* and then I thought, *I shouldn't eat a bagel because I don't want to have anything stuck in my teeth.* Sheldon Harnick and Joel were there. I took a bunch of 'family photos' with people I had never met, and that was that.

The most memorable note I got from Joel was during the rehearsal process for our second run, for the uptown transfer. He was giving notes for "Matchmaker" and he looked at me and said, "Don't be cute." I guess I was stressed because I just started crying — tears down my face. I think it was just kind of a release. I realized that I was good enough without putting something on. He said that I just need to want what I want and that I don't need to be cute because I already am. I'm someone who is naturally very smiley onstage, and it's not always because I'm playing a character but just because I'm happy to be on stage. That just reminded me to let myself *be* on stage. It's something I try to always remember when I'm acting.

* * *

Zalmen Mlotek

Musical Director

Joel Grey was the first one we had to get on the team. I purposely asked Joel because I had worked with him before, and I wanted to attach a big name to what I sensed would capture the interest of the general public. After Joel agreed to do it, I knew it would be important for him to work with a choreographer who knew the piece. Staś Kmieć reached out to me, and after realizing how perfect he was for the engagement, I suggested Staś to Joel. Joel also realized what a plus it would be to have someone like Staś on board, who has been involved in many Fiddler productions. For designers, Joel called on colleagues from the Broadway world and had them all come down to the museum. Everyone who came down to the museum didn't know what to expect, but they just fell in love with it. The theatre in the Museum of Jewish Heritage, which overlooks the Statue of Liberty and Ellis Island, resonated deeply for Joel and all the designers who visited as they considered Joel's invitation. As soon as you walk into that theatre, you feel the intimacy and how connected one can be to the audience and the stage. The designers all came on board. We were blessed to have Beowulf Boritt design our set, Peter Kaczorowski design the lighting, Ann Hould-Ward design the costumes, and Dan Moses Schreier sound design.

Then Joel, Beowulf, Peter, and Annie met by themselves to think about what the concept would be — how the production would look and feel. I remember the very first day that they invited me to the studio to see the diorama. I was so excited and I had no idea what to expect. When I first saw it, I thought to myself: *That's it? That's all?* Then I quickly realized what the concept was: to let the text, acting, and music transport us — presented as simply and starkly as possible. They wisely realized one couldn't compete with the mind's eye of the many versions on Broadway, in film, and all over the world, and had to come up with something completely unique. The word "Torah" was written in Hebrew on a huge sheet of crumpled paper, to simulate parchment. As soon as I saw that, I realized the power of that one word on this parchment and became emotional realizing how powerful it was. Then they told me about the concept of ripping it in the pogrom at the end of the act and I was 'sold.'

When we first announced the auditions, we were overwhelmed. We had twenty-five hundred inquiries, through which Jamibeth Margolis, our casting director, and us whittled down whom we would see. We saw seven hundred people. It was grueling, time consuming, and a strange process because we were looking for the actor, singer, dancer, and the quality of stage-worthyness, or the excitement of being on stage. On top of that, we needed people with an ear for Yiddish. There was a very small percentage of Yiddish or German speakers who could do it, so we had the audition sides recorded on the website so actors who didn't speak Yiddish could listen and learn them. After the first audition, if we felt that an actor did well with the Yiddish, we would give them more to learn. It was an interesting process in the audition room, because we would see someone sing and dance and we would love them, and then we would have to test their ear for the language. They would do the Yiddish, and we would have to tell Joel if we thought we could work with them or not. Sometimes it was very disappointing, because we saw some great candidates who just couldn't get the Yiddish. Joel was very patient and understanding right from the beginning. We all knew that the way the New York audience was going to perceive the Yiddish had to be honest and absolutely perfect.

Before we had our first day of rehearsal, we brought

our cast in for a big Yiddish coaching. We ran through all the music, and it was the first time we were hearing it all. Everyone was so excited to do it, and the cast came in almost entirely off book with the music. That was so thrilling to me, and I realized that the rehearsal process was just going to be about fine-tuning the Yiddish and the musical phrasing. People were so ready to do it. We have a very special company. The cast is incredibly talented, of course, but on top of that the way everyone works together is so beautiful. It's just a tribute to everybody's commitment.

I realized that the first day of rehearsal was going to be a major event, so I invited Sheldon Harnick and Elisa Stein, widow of Joe Stein, to be there, because I wanted them to share in the excitement of the moment. I also invited Hal Prince, who couldn't come that first day, but was an important guide to me from the moment I decided to do it. We all gathered on the stage to hear the opening number, which was originally "Di Toyre." *Fiddler on the Roof* is an incredibly well-constructed theatrical piece — one of the classics of musical theatre. The Yiddish element gives it this special appeal and extra truth behind it. I always pay homage to Sheldon Harnick, and Joseph Stein, Jerry Bock, Jerome Robbins, and Hal Prince — the team that first came up with it all. I had been in touch with Hal Prince from the very beginning, having gotten his input on thinking about a director for the show, and who to bring into the team. It was pretty wonderful when he came to see the show. He was traveling for a while, but when he finally made it, he was so excited and very enthusiastic about our production, graciously giving us an incredible quote that I asked him for: "If you have seen Fiddler before, you must see this production because it will make you feel you are seeing Fiddler for the first time." Getting the affirmation of all these creators has been very gratifying.

People ask me if I get tired of conducting this show, but the truth is that I never do. I never don't want to go to work. I always want to do this. It's not to say I don't get tired when doing two shows in a day, but the score is so rich and the piece is so good, and we have this excitement of knowing that people are coming to watch our production because they have heard great things about it. The audiences are alive, and very much there with us. We never know what the future holds in terms of how long this experience is going to be, but it's amazing that we are still here.

Part Two
Kvell

Sammy

Role: Beylke

On the first day of rehearsal, on June 4th, 2018, I woke up early to curl my hair, and I put on my light pink velvet overalls over my white and pink sweater. I packed my backpack with my notebook, water bottle, unicorn pencil case, and the *Tevye the Dairyman* book that my teacher Randy Graff had passed on to me from reading in preparation of her *Fiddler* debut in 2003. I practiced rolling my "r"s, as I had taught myself to do over the past few weeks, and listened to a happy playlist of songs on the hour-long subway ride down to Battery Park. I stopped at the end of the path through the archway of trees to stare up at the beautiful Museum of Jewish Heritage, inside of which stood the National Yiddish Theatre Folksbiene. I looked at my phone and saw that I was about thirty minutes early, so I started walking extremely slowly. I realized that if anyone saw me, they would immediately think I was either very weird or had some sort of a leg injury, so I gave up on being on time and quickly walked inside. I went through the security line and approached the front desk to ask where the *Fiddler* rehearsal was being held. They were still setting up the room, so I sat down on one of the huge benches in the lobby. I was, embarrassingly, the first one there, but it seemed fitting because I was the youngest one in the cast and a bit too excited to care. People started trickling in, and I recognized some of their faces from the Israeli Day Parade event that we were invited to attend, and the pre-rehearsal music session with Zalmen Mlotek, our musical director. I had no idea what any of their names were, though, and I was barely certain that they were from *Fiddler*. Then, in walked the oldest of the sisters, Rachel Zatcoff, in a long, striped romper with a beautiful jacket that was covered in buttons. We had met at the parade and music session, and I pretty much thought that she was the coolest person ever — I still do, in so many ways. She came right over to warmly greet me, and suddenly we were all heading into the rehearsal room.

The windowsills were lined with bagels and fruit, and the walls were lined with photo-backdrops. There were press agents everywhere, snapping pictures of everything. The cast, crew, creative team, designers, and even Sheldon Harnick and Elisa Stein were hugging and meeting each other all around the room. Joel Grey walked in and started greeting each person individually, as if we all were already a family. He caught my eye while he was hugging one of the guys, and I smiled at him sheepishly because I had just in that moment realized how hungry I was and stuffed half a bagel in my face. He said, "Come here, you silly thing," and gave me a big hug. I said nothing, of course, because I had a mouth full of bagel, but I happily hugged him back. The press agents started asking groups of people for pictures — we took hundreds of them. I am smiling so hard in every single one of those pictures; I seriously look like a rocket about to take off. When I wasn't taking photos, I was in a whirlwind of people and didn't know who to talk to. Then, I met a girl with beautiful blonde curls who seemed much closer to my age. I said, "Did you get your picture taken yet?"

She shyly replied, "No, not really."

I said, "Well, come on, let's get your picture taken! They are taking a bunch!"

Then she said, "Well, actually, would you mind taking one of me? Just to send to my mom?" We had a fun little photo session and clung to each other the rest of the day.

After the "meet and greet" portion, we all moved to the stage where they had set up a semi-circle of folding chairs for the designer presentation. Standing on the stage and looking out at the hundreds of seats, I felt goosebumps all over. This was my first time on an Off-Broadway stage, and in less than a month I would be performing on it. I grabbed a seat next to my new buddy Jodi: the brilliant actress who plays Frume Sore, and now one of my dearest friends. We went around the room and everyone stood up and introduced themselves;

then the designers each talked about their visions for the show. Zalmen shared a few elegant words about his excitement for the project and then humbly took his seat. Staś stepped up and buoyantly paid tribute to Jerome Robbins with his choreographed vision. Then Joel made a beautiful speech that had everyone smiling giddily in their seats. To close off the designer presentation, the entire company sang the opening number, "Tradition." There was excitement in the air — we could tell it was the start of something special.

The cast, stage management, and directors went back to the rehearsal room as the rest of the *Fiddler* crew left for the day. We had a short break, in which I dreamily surveyed the costume board from closer up, and then we received our scripts and started our first table-read of *Fiddler*. I was sitting next to Raquel on my left, who was excitedly chatting with me before we began, and Jackie Hoffman on my right, who was dryly whispering the most hilarious jokes in my ear throughout the entire read. The first read-through was one of the most special memories. We all laughed, wept, and cheered over hearing the poignant script from the mouths of our new family.

* * *

Jodi Snyder

Role: Frume Sore | Ensemble | Khave, Shprintze, Beylke Understudy

I've always wanted to do a production of *Fiddler on the Roof*. When an opportunity came up to try to audition for two different Fiddlers, I made sure I was first in line. I woke up incredibly early to put my name in for the Yiddish *Fiddler* EPA and the *Fiddler* tour audition, which were at different locations. I was number three at the tour and fourteen at this one. I was waiting at the tour and someone said, "they've seen all the EMC at the other Fiddler." I just thought, *Crap.* So I stayed at the tour, figuring my chances were better there, but tried to run back and forth a little. After running between them four times, I didn't get seen at either audition all day. I felt so defeated. My cousin emailed me that night saying, "You need to audition for this Joel Grey *Fiddler on the Roof*" to which I replied, "I'm literally trying." I gave up and thought it wasn't meant to be. The next day I was getting on a flight to Chicago to go home and I thought, *Maybe I'll audition in Chicago and if I don't find work for another year maybe I'll move there.* So the next morning I bring my suitcase to work with me at SoulCycle. I was working from five thirty to nine thirty in the morning and then later would catch my twelve thirty flight. At the end of my shift a friend called me and said, "I'm at the Fiddler ECC and they're seeing

33

Non-Union. You have to get here." Luckily, I'm twenty blocks away, so I *run* with my suitcase, in my leggings and gym shoes and no makeup. When I get there, I'm shocked that I made it and my heart is pounding. I throw on boots from my suitcase and change my shirt and hop into line. I was miraculously seen and made it to my twelve thirty flight. A few weeks and two callbacks later, I went to see a screening of "Schindler's List" with my cousin. I was sitting there watching it and thought, *Wouldn't it be so funny if I found out that I got "Fiddler" while watching this movie?* I came home from the movie and couldn't sleep all night but for some reason I didn't think to check my email. The next morning, I opened my email and saw that I booked the role of Frume Sore and that it had been in my inbox since the night before.

I definitely have moments from the rehearsal process where I remember thinking, *It's such a shame we aren't doing this in English.* It's funny because I feel the exact opposite now. The Yiddish is what makes it so special, fun, authentic, and challenging. Figuring out new choices has a whole new meaning when you don't have language on your side, which is really fun. I've learned more about listening, physical choices, and communication. During rehearsal I remember wondering if it was all going to come together. l wasn't always called, and when I was, we seemed to just be running the opening number "Tradition" a million times. For Frume, we only went up maybe five to ten times before previews. That sounds like a lot now that I'm saying it, but when it was so new to me it felt like we should do it a lot more. I also could not stop laughing when I was on top of Evan Mayer, because I'm afraid of heights, which is not something they ask you in the audition room. They don't say: "Oh, and if you were to play Frume Sore you would obviously be this many feet in the air…" I'm an actor so I'll jump in and do a lot of things, but I had no idea what was in store for Frume Sore. I ride on top of a man: I sit on top of Evan like a basic girl on top of a guy in her ripped jean shorts and tube top at a concert. Except we do that under a ten-pound dress while he runs, kicks, spins, and sometimes jumps. He's doing dance moves while I'm squeezing my inner thighs for dear life. I'm also moving my arms, thinking in English, singing in Yiddish, trying not to fall, and working plastic hands. Oh, and acting; I try to act too. I could not stop giggling during the rehearsal because I was a little scared and also, I wasn't used to it and I just thought it was the funniest sensation ever. Luckily, I pulled it together for the first time Joel saw it because I was scared out of my pants for that. Over the course of this production, I've had three bottoms. All of my bottoms, my legs — we talk about how we really become *one*. We communicate a lot during those three minutes. I'll squeeze my legs, he'll grab more; I'll hop on more, he'll hold on tighter. We definitely can feel what each other is thinking and feeling.

Every time we had a meeting downtown, talking

about the future of the show, I was just dumbfounded. I would sit there confused and crying. I never really thought this would be big at all and it was so amazing to feel the success of the show with everyone else. I kept trying to line other jobs up just in case and I would be really close to getting them, but they never worked out. I slowly started to realize there was a reason for that, because I can't imagine what my life would have been like if I had left this show and not gotten to experience what an amazing journey it is turning out to be. Every part of being in this show has been so bashert. From the audition to now, everything has felt meant to be.

* * *

Evan Mayer

Role: Sasha | Ensemble | Perchik, Der Gradavoy Understudy

Working with Jodi Snyder, my Fruma, has simply been the best. What we are doing is the ultimate partnering experience. I've never had to do something so hard in a show, and I couldn't imagine doing it with anyone else. We connected on day one downtown, before we even knew that I was going to be her "Fruma-bottom." We couldn't get through a rehearsal of "Tradition" or "Sabbath Prayer" without looking at each other and cracking up. I've honestly never laughed so hard as when we did the run, in front of everyone in Ripley Grier Studios. I'm honestly surprised we didn't get separated. Developing what Frume Sore was going to be with her was an incredible experience. We would go into the costume department, and she would be up on my shoulders for fifteen minutes, and then we would go into the rehearsal room and figure out how we could turn in circles and what we needed to do to move together. It feels like our little mark on the show and it is so fun to do that. Every time we had a tough rehearsal or a long costume fitting, our tradition became getting dollar ice cream cones at McDonald's. Ice cream cured everything.

I will always remember opening night and the emotions that came with it. The nerves were so high, and I was so anxious that my mouth was twitching during the opening number. I couldn't stop smiling and I felt like a jittery mess. After the bottle dance was over, I remember all four of us bottle dancers taking the deepest sigh of relief. It was the most euphoric release ever, and when we got to the end of the number, we were all beaming with joy. Now that we have done over a hundred shows uptown, we have a lot of backstage traditions that have evolved. Before the show, I do eight minutes of abs with whomever is free to join. Then I warm up in the house with Jodi, John Quigley, Steven Skybell and others. The dressing room is a full-on party before the show, with different DJs every day. We listen to everything from country to Britney Spears, and even

"Sesame Street." We have little rituals we do during every show too. Our stage manager Kat and I share a cute little moment in "Tradition" when I come on as the priest and we do a little hand jive. We have a joke circle before "The Dream" that started with Jodi, Rachel Zatcoff, Ben Liebert, and me when everyone else was onstage. Now it has grown and the dressers have joined us. Everyone goes around and tells a joke, which can be a dad joke or a crude joke or a long joke, and it's a really fun mid-show connection. Mikhl and I fool around before the "Tradition Crossover" and talk in weird British accents. Nick and I share a funny moment right before entering where we mouth to each other "I don't think so."

Leaving this show in the fall to work on another show and coming back five months later gave me a lot of perspective. It confirmed how special this group of people is, and how important it is to tell this story. When I left the downtown production and everyone sang "Happy Trails", I remember saying how musical theatre can sometimes seem superfluous. Singing and dancing can feel unimportant when there are so many problems in our world, but doing this show proved to me exactly how powerful musical theatre can be. It has been so powerful feeling the energy from our audiences, and hearing from our audience members who come backstage. It has affected me deeply as well. The friendships I have made here will last a lifetime. There has never been a group like this. We are truly a family.

We band together and with that sense of community have learned all the things we can accomplish. That's something you don't get with every show. I just feel so happy and honored to be a part of such a wonderful group of people.

Part Three
Kvetch

Sammy

Role: Beylke

To get into the ethos of our Anatevka characters, we were told to come to rehearsal with shmatas tied around our hair, long rehearsal skirts, and no makeup. This quickly became referred to as our "shtetl-chic" look. Some wore it gracefully: Rachel Zatcoff in a colorful shmata and patterned wrap-skirt to pair with her cute tank tops and T-shirts. Others, namely myself, brought in their roommate's scarf to messily twist around their head for the first choreography rehearsal. Luckily, I had Amazon Prime and quickly ordered myself a normal shmata, which I suddenly had a gaggle of older sisters to help me tie. Stephanie Lynne Mason, the second oldest of the sisters, gleefully taught me how to properly wear a shmata — the first of many lessons from my incredible show sisters. We all took turns holding each other's hair, as we still do in the dressing rooms sometimes.

Rehearsal was in a large, open classroom at the Museum of Jewish Heritage, just across the hallway from the theatre. The hallway was covered in affecting photographs from the museum, which to me seemed to serve as a daily reminder of the history we were portraying with our story of *Fiddler*. On one side of the classroom were high, thin windows with cabinets underneath, in which we stored our belongings. On the other side were tables where stage management and our directors sat — far too close for comfort when working on a scene. The stage management table fascinated me though; I loved the endless supply of tissues, hand sanitizer, cough drops, and multi colored tape that perched in front of their binders and laptops. More than that, I loved how every so often Joel Grey would toddle over to the stage management table and carefully unwrap a lemon cough drop to place in his mouth, as if Ricola was the finest of delicacies. Joel brought in a huge banner that said, "Fiddish Spoken Here," meaning *Fiddler* Yiddish, and hung it on the wall for us all to sign.

The first number we staged was the opening number, "Tradition." Staś Kmieć started the rehearsal by having us get into a big circle, which took up most of the room. He gave us a speech about "tradition": how important it is to our characters, and how much heart, pride, and community is encapsulated in the word. Joel asked us to really consider what the word "tradition" meant to each one of our characters. We started learning the classic arm-pumping motion of "Tradition" while simply walking around the room to get a feel for the action. Staś explained that the pulse comes from the chest— the heart center; that is where all the pride and love for our shtetl emanates from. We walked around in circles, pumping our arms for long enough that everyone was either thinking: *what the heck are we doing?* or *I think my arms are going to fall off*.

When we broke for lunch, wondering what the heck we had just accomplished, the cast headed outside to eat. The sun was shining on the two picnic tables outside of the museum, which became our cozy little lunch spot. I had packed my lunch — a responsibility I all too quickly abandoned as soon as I found out that the deli down the street made a delicious and reasonably priced grilled cheese sandwich. The packers went straight to the tables, and the buyers trickled in later, describing their food purchases to the ogling table of people. We didn't have to make as much awkward chatter as I had imagined; in fact, our lunch time flew right by. We immediately bonded and laughed over the ridiculousness of the never-ending arm-pumping we had just done, and it seemed to me like we were all already some sort of little family.

Later on, we headed back to the rehearsal room and learned the real choreography for "Tradition." The number starts with us all holding hands and stomping in unity: walking onto the stage as one big, proud shtetl. To me, that is exactly what we have always felt like. We made eye contact across the circle and squeezed each other's hands just for the fun of it. We bickered amongst ourselves over the best way to keep track of how many pulses we did before we were supposed to stop — a detail that is so second nature to us now that I can't even remember how we pinpointed it. We all laughed hysterically when Staś stopped to work on the turns with us and Jackie Hoffman exclaimed, "Every turn is a bane!" We delighted in the small vignettes as we saw each other's characters come to life for the first time. We all revelled in the beauty, anticipation, frustration, excitement, and joy of learning the opening number with our entire cast. I went home that night and took a shower, put on my pajamas, turned out the lights, and crawled into bed. A minute later I got out of bed, turned on the lights, took the pillow case off of my pillow to wrap around my head like a shmata, and practiced the "Tradition" choreography. Even in my little bedroom, wearing my *Yertle the Turtle* hand-me-down pajama shirt and my blue pillow case around my head — it felt like I was doing something special.

* * *

Staś Kmieć

Choreographer

I fell in love with *Fiddler* when I was eleven years old, when I saw the film version. I went to Poland that year for the first time to visit some distant relatives, and they lived on a farm with a well, cows, and chickens — very similar to how Tevye's family lives. *Fiddler* became one of my favorite musicals, and it has always been very close to me since then. For a while I never had the opportunity to be involved in a production of *Fiddler*, until I finally got cast in the national tour with Theodore Bikel. I got to do all of the Russian dances, and the "bottle dance." I loved it, and I stayed with that production for two years. Then the same director set the St. Louis Muny in Kansas City Starlight production of Fiddler and asked if I was available, so I performed in that next. Five years later, I went on another tour of Fiddler. There were also other Fiddlers I was involved in along the way at different playhouses. Then I started setting them everywhere — sometimes as a choreographer, sometimes as a director/choreographer. For the most part I stuck to the original Jerome Robbins choreography. I was very loyal to that, but when you do it on different people it looks differently, and I never want to pigeonhole anyone into it. It's a living, breathing piece, so it's about getting people to live and breathe within those confines.

In January 2018, I got a call from the Jerome Robbins Foundation telling me that this production of Yiddish *Fiddler* was going to happen, and that they were interested in having me as the choreographer. There wasn't a lot of back and forth on the conversation, and all I heard for months was crickets. I kept on writing to Zalmen Mlotek, asking if there was any follow-up happening on the project, and he kept saying, "Not yet." In March, Joel Grey got on board, and the show was announced on Paybill.com. The next day I got a call saying that Joel wanted to see me. I met with Joel and Zalmen, and we discussed the show. Joel said, "I know that you've done this before, but I'm looking at it to be different."

I replied, "I'm open to that. If anyone is going to do this differently, I think it should be me, because I know it so well." I knew that I could stay loyal to the show while making the changes. One of the first things he said was that he didn't want to do a "bottle dance." He thought it was too presentational, and too much of a showstopper. I still didn't have the job yet, so I said I was open to what he wanted to do but that we should discuss it further because it is a very pivotal piece. I explained the idea of the dance being a gift to the married couple and said we could talk about it more later on. We talked about many different things, and how we could do them differently, and then I left and got on the subway. When I got off of the subway, I had a phone call from Chris Massimine, our producer at the National Yiddish Theatre Folksbiene, offering me the job.

Joel and I met many times in his apartment after that. He made me espresso coffee, and we started off by using salt and pepper shakers as the people to move around and talk about the show with. We shared our views of the show with each other, and just started to get the dialogue flowing between us. We are sort of the yin and yang — we work off of each other. We met once or twice a week until it got to a point where I decided to draw up diagrams instead of using salt and pepper shakers. We talked it all through and got ourselves on a good foot for the first day of rehearsal in June.

I started by staging "Tradition" on the first day of rehearsal, because I think that is the number that provides the cast with a sense of community. It's the perfect starting number, because it's about the shtetl, and the relationships there. After that first day of rehearsal, I had no doubt that our Yiddish *Fiddler* was going to work. In interviews, people asked if we were worried about this production. Joel and Zalmen said yes, but I said "Nope! I knew from that first day of working on "Tradition." I used about ten times the amount of Russian dancing than the original choreography ever had. It exhilarates me to see the dancers perform it each night. After watching the show this many times, there are still many moments that excite me, like Nick Raynor's toe-touch and the pile up at the end of "To Life."

Working with Steven Skybell has been really incredible. Every time I gave him a little piece of something, he took it and came back and made it his own. He always went beyond my wildest dreams with what he was able to do. He worked on Rich Man with Joel, and there was a point when he was just sitting on the milk jug the entire time. I said we had to move him around more, and I gave him movements to use the entire stage, but stay in character. It was giving Joel's internal ideas a physical framework. There is one move that particularly reminds me of my grandfather, and every time I see Steven do it, it feels really special.

One of my favorite numbers is "The Dream," because it's like a playground and it's so different than anything else in the show. It's fun, funny, and crazy, and I really enjoyed playing with it. We did the piece very differently than it has been done before, with the use of shadows and the hand that comes down and plucks Bobe Tsaytl away before Frume Sore's entrance. I had so much fun with it. Everyone was saying it wasn't going to work, and I was told to abandon it before I even started it, but I knew it could work. Joel had an idea to do the entire number in shadows. Then Ann Hould-Ward, the costume designer, asked if we wanted puppets, which I said no to. I told them that the number couldn't work in just shadows, and that it had to be coming out of the shadows for the story to be told. The audience needs to be able to fully see Frume Sore for the number to make sense. From that, the magic was achieved in having all of the characters come out of the shadows until Frume Sore enters the scene and the kabuki curtain drops entirely. The whole process was about collaborating and playing with people's ideas.

In regards to the "bottle dance," I had told Joel I would stage the dance and show it to him, and if he didn't like it, it would be cut. It was a gamble. Unbeknownst to the dancers, I taught them the entire dance, but did not let them know of the circumstances. I made changes in dynamic, focus, and nuance to give it even greater life. Once I set the wedding scene, we showed Joel everything in context. After the "bottle dance," he looked over to me and gave me a thumbs up to signify that it was staying in the show.

A favorite memory of mine was our first preview performance for an audience. Everyone was a little on-edge, and a lot of the cast was focused on just remembering their lines. There was this unique energy and simplicity in it that I keep trying to remind us of, because everyone was so focused on getting the Yiddish right and remembering everything from the short rehearsal process. It was so energized, focused, and real.

* * *

Mikhl Yashinsky

Role: Nokhum | Mordkhe | Mendl Understudy

When I was in town to play the title role in *The Sorceress* with the National Yiddish Theatre Folksbiene, many of the actors met each other the night before our first rehearsal at the company's annual gala. At that event, our cherished artistic director Zalmen Mlotek announced to the audience that the summer production would be *Fidler Afn Dakh*. Joel Grey hadn't been announced as the director yet, but I knew I wanted terribly to be a part of *Fiddler on the Roof in Yiddish.* I was living in Amherst, Massachusetts at the time, working on Yiddish research, translation, and pedagogy at the Yiddish Book Center, while coming into the city every now and then for gigs. I bused in for the audition for *Fiddler.* A part of me hoped Joel Grey would not be in the audition room because I so revered him as a performer, having seen *Cabaret* as a boy and being in wonderment forever after at what a dynamic, unusual, magnetic talent he had. I was scared about seeing him in that small audition room, but when I walked in the room and saw him grinning, his energy made me feel instantly at ease. As soon as I saw that he was this kindly gentleman with a big smile on his face, laughing as I did my monologue for the part of Mordkhe the Innkeeper, I felt *heymish.* That means, "at home." I had a feeling then, and I've come to know now, what a charming, wonderfully impish sort he is. We are a joyful cast and I think a lot of that joy comes from him.

For the callback, I bused in again, and was there in the room with a whole group of guys, hoping with all my being to make it through to the end. I knew Yiddish coming into it, so that element was only thrilling, not stressful. What was stressful was caring so deeply about this project, and wanting so much be a part of it. Like any decent American Jew, I have always loved *Fiddler*; I also played Tevye as a high school junior. My dear Yiddishist grandmother, Elizabeth Elkin Weiss, was also an actress and owned an Israeli cast recording of *Fiddler* in Yiddish. Because of this, I had known of its glories for a long time, and the need to be in this show felt like a pressing demand upon my very soul. I was at my friend Liz's housewarming party back in Massachusetts when I got the email with the offer for *Fiddler*, and I sort of halted the proceedings of the party to read it out loud. Everyone went wild, and I loved them for it. It was the wee hours of the morning when I got home so it was too late to text my mother back and tell her the news. When I woke the next day, I just texted her a violin emoji. She knew what that meant and called me immediately, crying — just as happy as I was.

The first day of rehearsal, after the somewhat awkward photo-op with all of the press agents, was very special. We gathered onstage to sing through the opening number, *"Traditsye,"* for the first time. Sheldon Harnick, Joe Stein's widow Elisa Stein, Joel, Zalmen, and our talented and knowledgeable choreographer Staś Kmieć were all there, as well as the whole cast and crew and the designers of the production. We sang

through it, and it starts so rousingly that I think we could all just feel it in our bones: with that lilting fiddle and those glorious bangs on the drums, we knew what a special thing this was going to be. Of course at that time we weren't singing "Traditsye," we were singing "Di toyre." "Di toyre" was how the original translator Shraga Friedman rendered the title, feeling it was a more Jewish way of thinking about what encapsulates our "tradition": the Torah. From the days when I had first heard the Tel Aviv cast singing it on my grandma's vinyl, I always thought that was such a lovely and interesting choice, but it wasn't one we ended up going with.

There are certain musical moments in the show that still get to me, even after so many performances. I love the bits where the music ramps up to the next level and it's just this unbridled, uniquely Jewish joy. This is something that gets forgotten a bit as the show ends, after all of the Jewish tragedy of Act Two — all those precious moments of Jewish joy. In "Lekhaim," after all the singing is done and it's just mad, fevered dancing, I always feel the percussionist and the guitarist just going at it, like we're at a rock concert in the Pale of Settlement circa 1905. It's thrilling. We also get that in the wedding dance where the orchestra lets loose, and the music fills us with a certain wild vigor as we whirl about. Staś always tells us to shout as much as we can throughout various moments like that — just bellow rapturous exclamations in Yiddish. It is good for the spirit, if not for the vocal cords.

I take part in this rather strenuous dance in the wedding called "Whips and Hooks." It's inspired by dancing Jerome Robbins witnessed at a Hasidic wedding in Brooklyn, where he saw men letting themselves go in a wild abandon, working themselves up into a kind of ecstasy by giving themselves over to dance and to song. They let that then move their spirit in the classic Hasidic manner. It is great fun, even if rather difficult to go straight from it into my long and spirited wedding speech that follows — welcoming the guests, honoring the bride and groom, presenting the wedding gifts, and so forth, without pausing for a breath. During "Whips and Hooks," on the other side of the partition between the men and women, the ladies are doing something equally interesting to me. I can only see it out of the corner of my eye as I fling myself about, but it looks like the small-gestured, even, somewhat slow-moving dances that you see the elaborately frocked women doing at wedding scenes as staged in Yiddish films of the 1930s, like *Yidl mitn fidl*. It is restrained but joyful, with the joy coming from within.

There are little moments of action onstage that are always a laugh for me, too. I'm discovering new ones all the time, both that my fellow actors are doing and ones that come to me. I try to let my performance be very mutable — responding to new energies in the house, on the stage, and in my mind and heart. When we moved uptown, I was discussing with my castmate and dressing-room neighbor Kirk Geritano if there was anyone onstage that we never have any interaction with. I realized that Samantha Hahn, who plays Beylke, was the one person in the show that I never had a single moment with — not one handclasp, look, or word. Over time that changed, and now as the men lift up the chuppah in the wedding, we have a bit where we share our excitement about how high and beautiful the billowing of the cloth is. I'm very glad we have that, and that I now interact onstage with every one of my castmates and friends. A lot of these moments come as we all watch the bottle dance. I turn to Drew Seigla, who plays Perchik, and we have a bit of shtik pretending I'm teaching him how one accompanies the dancers because he is the new arrival to our shtetl. I say, "Itst knaklen mir! An anatevker mineg!" This means, "Now we snap! An Anatevka custom!" It's something the audience likely does not notice, but for us it adds a level of realness and authentic communication onstage. It is a feeling that we are inhabiting our parts and this shtetl, just as the Yiddish language does for us so richly and usefully. In the same scene, when I go over to conduct the women in the "yay-day-day"s by waving about my handkerchief, Jackie Hoffman, as Yente, either plays at trying to catch the handkerchief or being somehow hypnotized by it. So many bits like this bring me a special contentment. There's even a scene-change that gets me: when Stephanie Lynne Mason, as Hodl, moves Motl's dress form into place before the scene called "Tailor Shop 1." She does it with such a characteristic, "Stephanie-ish" poise, and also a bit of a smile like Hodl is very proud and happy to be helping out around the shop, or maybe like she is thinking of her beloved Perchik. It's a tiny thing, but it gladdens my heart. One must keep finding little things to gladden the heart and lift the spirit after doing a show so many times.

It is also fun to see the actors playing around with

the language more as they've gotten more comfortable with it. I'm always happy to provide Yiddish adlibs when people approach me backstage and ask how they would put something in a certain moment. I would never give notes to anyone, but it pleases me to help out when they come to me with questions. Likewise, it pleases me to see the cast becoming more and more interested in the culture and the language beyond just the script of the show. Taking that interest is important to us as people, and to the performance. We should always remember what we are doing onstage, what story we are telling, and what history we are enacting. At the end of our original summer run, a number of people who had other gigs waiting left the show for a while. I left to take up a position teaching Yiddish at the University of Michigan. The company and crew sang "Happy Trails" to us and asked us to speak. I was moved to say something like, "Never forget the actual people that inhabited this place and time that we are inhabiting onstage. Keep learning. Keep remembering." It is so important to keep in our hearts and minds the joys, sorrows, and the suffering of the real people of that time. The pogroms, the Holocaust and the six million martyrs, and the millions more who lived quiet and passionate and loving lives in Yiddish, in Ashkenazic Europe for a millennium, are all a part of this story we are telling. Now we are a part of that story, too, that *goldene keyt*, which means "golden chain" of cultural transmission that we have now taken hold of, and have the honor of grasping and holding up high onstage. Our Yiddish *Fiddler* is not just a show or a job; it's linked to our hearts, as we are all linked to each other, and to the people of centuries past whose stories we are telling.

Also, on that last night of the summer, Josh Dunn, another member of our original cast who was leaving, and I did a farewell dance with each other in the dressing room. We started out with the backward-jerking motion of "Whips and Hooks," but then instead of hooking our arms and swinging about, we just grabbed hold of each other, and spun about in each other's embrace. "Whips and Hugs," we called it: an apt farewell dance for *Fiddler*. Tears and laughter, sunshine and sorrow, and whips and hugs.

* * *

Kirk Geritano

Role: Avrom | Motl, Leyzer-Volf, Nokhum/Mordkhe Understudy

Mandy Patinkin came backstage and talked to us after he saw the show. He told us that when he was doing *Sunday in the Park with George* it was just his daily job. Every day he went in, did what he had to do, and then left. After the show closed, he was driving in his car and listening to their cast recording and he had to pull over because he was so emotional about what he was hearing.

He didn't realize in the moment what he had with that show. Hearing the cast album again brought him the realization that they had something really special. He told us this story so he could make sure to impart to us that what we have is very special. We should hold onto it, never forget it, and always be in the moment and appreciate it. That really helps me keep perspective on what we are doing here and how it is so important.

There are other memorable moments that aren't as moving, like when an audience member let out a very loud burp right in the quiet moment in the middle of "L'Chaim." "L'Chaim" is my favorite part of the show because we get to just exude all this joy. The Russians and the Jews are all dancing together and having fun. It's the one moment in the musical where there's no tension, and it's just a bunch of human beings celebrating together. I play Avrom, the bookseller. I view him as the chicken little of the shtetl. He's very excitable, and he's a little paranoid about what's happening in the outside world. He has a vivid imagination because he reads a lot and comes up with his own stories. When he goes off the deep end a bit, it is just because everything is so vivid and clear to him. My favorite part of being in this show is how historical it is and how much it means to people. Being able to impart that to other people and being able to bring Yiddish into the mainstream is very cool. We get to allow people to reminisce and relate to the universality of this story, which is very cool.

Working with Joel is very intimidating at the start because you're a little star- struck by him. His stature as a person and artist is so big and commanding. After a while you realize he is also a down-to-earth human being who has such a great personality and is fun to be around. Something amazing about him is that he always sits down and tells people how good somebody else is so that they'll go to that person and say, "Do you know what Joel Grey just said about you?" During the cast recording he told me, "Jen is fantastic. Jen is a star." Of course I went to Jen Babiak and told her that he said that, and it just made her day. It's really cool how he does that. He's always here too — he didn't just direct the show and leave. He comes back and is very personable and warm and it's really great to have him around.

Part Four
Shvesterlekh

Sammy

Role: Beylke

We went to Ripley Grier Studios for a few of the early rehearsals in the middle of June 2018: days that are unlikely to lose their vividness in my memories for the foreseeable future. The first thing on my rehearsal schedule was "Matchmaker" with Joel Grey. Joel brought me, Raquel, Rosie, Stephanie, and Rachel into a rehearsal room and had us start talking through the "Matchmaker" lyrics in English. We spoke the whole song in English, and then Joel started asking us questions. He went around and asked each of us about our characters: who they are, how they feel about their sisters, how they feel about boys, etc. Raquel talked about being stuck as a middle sister, Rosie discussed the things she reads about boys in her books, Stephanie explained that she wants only the best man, and Rachel described her adoration of her childhood best friend, and her obligations as the oldest sister. I delighted in the insights of each of my scene mates, along with Joel's clarifying questions back and forth with them. I took a hard "no boys" stance and shared my feelings of being the youngest of the five sisters, saying, "I'm a little left out of the gossip, but my sisters like to baby me which is fun because I get a lot of attention." Joel nodded thoughtfully at my remarks and then turned to the other girls and asked, "Do you like to baby her? Is she like your little doll?" to which my show sisters happily said, "Oh, yes!" When we started to talk through the English version of the scene again, Joel frequently stopped us to ask questions about the moments and what we were saying.

We had a similar process when Joel brought Golde, who was originally played by the lovely Mary Illes, into the room to work the first scene of the show with us. After making all of these discoveries in English, Joel would say, "Again! Now in Yiddish." If while saying the lines in Yiddish we lost any of the meaning or intention we had just found, he would stop the scene and ask us to say the line in English again. We went back and forth from doing it in English to doing it in Yiddish, continually being stopped by Joel with thought-provoking questions. It was the most collaborative process of discovery. It was also the most frustrating and challenging process ever, because we were constantly switching languages and never allowed to make it through the entire scene without Joel stopping us. Our brains were so exhausted from constantly switching gears, that towards the end of the rehearsal people started accidentally saying their lines in Yiddish while we were running the scene in English, and vice versa. It felt like the most confusing thing in the world, but it grew us exponentially. We thought our minds were failing us, but, really, we were learning to think in Yiddish and English at the same time.

When it was time to stage the scene, Joel didn't give us any specific blocking. He said, "Okay, let's put it on its feet. Just... talk to each other, and go where you want to go. Let's just see what happens." We entered the scene over and over again, stumbling around and slowly finding our way. We tried out doing different activities like cleaning, cooking, playing, and fixing each other up for Shabbos; there were no props or sets yet, so we could play around with whatever we wanted to. Whatever choices we made, Joel challenged us. He never told us we should or shouldn't do anything, in the beginning, but he asked pointed questions that made us reconsider any extraneous movements. This was the best blocking strategy an actor could imagine because every single move was inherently infused with strong intentions, and it was all coming from us.

On our last day at Ripley, we staged the monstrous scene known as Act One, Scene Six. Scene 1.6 starts off with Beylke and Shprintze having a Bible lesson with Perchik, continues through the first romantic encounter of Hodl and Perchik and the "Hodl-Perchik Dance," then the first "Rebuttal" with Tsaytl, Motl, and Tevye, in which Tsaytl refuses to marry Leyzer-Volf, and ends with "Miracle of Miracles," after Tevye gives Motl and

Tsaytl his blessing to be married. It is a huge scene packed with the highest stakes and emotions for several characters. It's also the longest scene in existence. Because of this, rehearsing the scene was a crazy, frustrating, difficult process.

I was excited about staging the scene that day, because it was one of my biggest moments in the show as the youngest daughter. Raquel and I sat on the floor facing upstage with Daniel Kahn, the original Perchik, perched on the end of the bench between us. We were listening to the "lesson" in the scene and waiting for our little lines and singing at the end, when out of the corner of my eye I saw Joel looking at me. I turned my head to get a quick look at him — he was pointedly tapping his thumbnail on his lower lip and staring at me. I quickly looked back at the scene that was still occurring, but kept peeking at Joel, completely confused as to what was going on. As the scene continued, I could still feel him looking at me, so I turned my head towards him again. This time, he was making a big motion of tapping his thumb to his mouth and nodding his head at me. I looked at him, confused, and did a quick 360 around the room, trying to figure out if anyone knew what the heck he was doing, because I had no clue. I turned back to the scene, and then cautiously raised my thumb to my lips. I started playing around with biting on my thumb while listening to the "lesson" from Perchik, and then peeked at Joel again, thinking: *Is this what you're trying to get me to do?* Suddenly Joel said, "Stop." We all turned to

61

look at him, and, of course, he was staring right at me. We locked eyes, and then he very deliberately put his thumb in his mouth. I just looked at him. He didn't say anything, he just tilted his head down ever so slightly and raised his eyebrows at me. I desperately wanted to turn around and see what everyone's expressions were in that moment, but all I could do was look at Joel, dumbfounded, and wearily put my thumb in my mouth. He started nodding, so I nodded back at him — both with our thumbs in our mouths. I turned back to the scene, thinking: *What just happened?* Out of nowhere, a rush of embarrassment came over me. *Was I going to have to get onstage in front of everyone who was so excited for me to be in this musical, only to be sucking my thumb? What kind of nine-year-old sucks their thumb anyway? Forget that — what kind of twenty-year-old should be sucking their thumb onstage?* I began to feel ashamed. I slowly started to pull back my thumb so it was only half in my mouth: twisting it around and trying to turn it into a more casual motion. Joel abruptly stopped us again, saying, "Put your whole thumb in your mouth. All the way. Just leave it there, like you enjoy it, like it's something you do." I shoved my thumb back in my mouth and turned beet red — that is how I remained for the rest of the rehearsal.

At the end of the rehearsal, my show sisters started talking about going to see a concert called "Yiddish Under The Stars" presented by the National Yiddish Theatre Folksbiene and City Parks Foundation in

Central Park. Jackie Hoffman was emceeing the concert, and Daniel Kahn was performing in it with his band, "The Painted Bird." The five of us were gathered in the hallway, and Stephanie offered that we all go to her apartment to kill time before the concert. Rosie asked me if I was coming or not, and I said, "Umm... I don't think so..." I was exhausted from the day, embarrassed and frustrated about the thumb sucking, and sporting frizzy hair and a sweaty, old *Pippin* T-shirt. It did not seem like the time to go to a concert with four older girls that I barely knew and at the same time already held in high regard. Then Raquel grabbed my arm and said, "She's coming!"

We all walked to the elevator, talking about what a crazy day of rehearsal it was. Rachel and Stephanie were also flustered from their 1.6 sessions, so I was in good company; their rehearsals were filled with high emotions, confusion, and cozy irritation. It was the longest week, and we all had so many mixed feelings boiling inside of us. The five of us got in the elevator, and when the doors closed Rachel said, "I feel like I need to scream or something." I said, "Actually, same."

Then Rosie said, "Should we scream?" Half a second later, all five of us were screaming at the top of our lungs on the elevator ride down in Ripley Grier Studios. As soon as the elevator dinged, we stopped screaming, and when the doors opened, we strolled out through the lobby like nothing had ever happened. Suddenly, all of my feelings about the rehearsal transformed — I was absolutely giddy. I was surrounded by four incredible, talented women and we were all in it together.

We walked a few blocks to Stephanie's apartment, where we drank wine, laughed, and talked about everything that had happened at rehearsal. Raquel, the friendly and inclusive, stylish girl sat across the room from me, starting charming conversations. Rosie, the funny dancer, sat next to her on the ground, throwing in crude quips and hilarious jokes. Stephanie, the caring and hospitable second-oldest, conversed while walking around the kitchen and making sure everyone had drinks. Rachel, the radiant, wise, and joyous oldest sister sat next to me on the couch, adding insights and stories and delighting in everyone's individuality. We ordered Domino's pizza which made us all feel sick, shared embarrassing memories, and got to know each other a lot better. I was pretty shy and less talkative than the others, but when I made a little joke that had Rachel laughing her face off and telling me that she quoted me to her husband, I beamed from the inside out.

We all went over to Central Park together, plopping on the grass to watch Jackie hilariously introduce the concert. We clapped and danced along with the amazing music until to our surprise, Mandy Patinkin came onstage to present Daniel Kahn with the Yosl and Chana Mlotek Memorial Prize for Yiddish Continuity. There were tears of joy, and, of course, we snuck our way up behind the stage to congratulate Dan and get a picture with Mandy Patinkin. It was near midnight when we said our goodbyes and parted ways on the outskirts of Central Park, feeling a new sense of bonded sisterhood. On the subway ride home, I marveled over the beautiful feeling of having four new older sisters, meeting Mandy Patinkin, and the memory of Joel Grey and me, staring at each other and sucking our thumbs in Ripley Grier Studios.

* * *

Stephanie Lynne Mason

Role: Hodl

I've done a lot of productions of *Fiddler*, but this is my favorite. This cast has a really special bond. The way everybody cares about every show and wants it to be the best it can be is just amazing. I like to bake treats to bring in for the cast during rehearsals and shows. I learned to cook from my mom and my grandmother when I was a kid. My grandmother used to have these parties where the motto was: "the more the merrier." Food definitely became a love language for me, and baking is a hobby of mine. I love to experiment with new recipes on this cast, and I love to cheer people up during a rough week of shows by bringing in my food. My favorite part of the show is "Matchmaker." We have a little huddle when all five of the sisters are together, and it makes me happy every night. I remember the first time that the five daughters all bonded outside of the theatre together. Rachel Zatcoff, Rosie Jo Neddy, Raquel Nobile, Samantha Hahn, and I all went to the "Yiddish Under The Stars" concert in Central Park toward the beginning of the rehearsal process downtown. Daniel Kahn, the original Perchik, was being presented an award, and we all went to watch together. We drank way too much wine, ate Domino's pizza, which hurt all of our stomachs, and we had an amazing night. That felt like the beginning of our sisterhood and it was very special to me.

Steven Skybell as our Tevye is such an incredible cast member. He is so truthful and he brings this positivity and light to everything he does, in life and onstage. It elevates the show to an entirely different level, and it's a trickle-down effect that radiates throughout the entire company. I think part of the reason why Steven Skybell is so good is that he has such a big heart and he is so open. He is so real in every moment, and he really reacts to anything you give him. I've never worked with such a dependable scene partner. Doing "Far From the Home I Love" with him is so amazing. He is one hundred percent there, he's got your back, and there is never a moment that feels put-on or fake.

The way Joel directed this show really turned my world upside down. He brought out the fact that Hodl is a strong woman. In the first scene of Act Two, I had always just seen Hodl as being really upset and sad. He helped me realize that she is strong in that moment, that she understands Perchik, and that she's actually trying to help him. In "Far from the Home I Love" it is Hodl who is strong and wants to make sure that her dad is okay. He brought a strength out of her and also out of me that I had completely forgotten about. Joel was tough on me, but he got my walls down and really enriched my life in a lot of ways, onstage and off. When I came into this show, I hadn't been in a relationship in a while, and I had gone through a really tough breakup. The way Joel directed Daniel Kahn, the original Perchik downtown, and me, kind of got my heart ready. He forced me to be honest as an actress, and also as a human. In telling the truth and slowly letting my guard down, it got me ready to experience love. I wasn't expecting Drew when he came along. We really connected. We were running lines one day, and we realized we had all of these things in common and it was just this innate chemistry. Sometimes it's hard if we get in an argument and we have to do these lovey-dovey scenes, but at the same time he is so professional, and we are such good scene partners that it isn't ever a problem. In real life we joke that I'm more of a Perchik and he's more of a Hodl, and Joel likes to say that he is our "Shadkhnte" which means "Matchmaker."

* * *

Drew Seigla

Role: Perchik

When I first entered into the company as the replacement for Perchik, I had just gotten out of an eight-year relationship. I was in need of support, and I found that in my new scene partner, Stephanie Lynne Mason. Stephanie was there to help me with the lines and help get me ready to step into the role of Perchik. She really wanted me to do as well as possible in the show, and she was always there to meet up before rehearsal to help me with the material. Through working together, we got to know each other really well and it blossomed into this really great trust. Shortly after my opening night, it was clear that we had grown to care for each other. Now, we are in love with each other. Being in a relationship in real life adds a lot of truthfulness and depth to our onstage relationship. We know how to pull out the best in each other onstage and offstage. Having her as a scene partner is wonderful because there is so much trust and we really have each other's backs; we're always there to catch each other if we stumble or fall.

Working with Joel Grey has been amazing. Joel has always told me to make things as simple and as honest as possible. This has been a huge lesson for me. In life, I have an instinct to be enthusiastic and big, which can breed erroneous gesticulations. Joel really helped me make everything as simple as possible. He made it all about the eye contact, and connecting with my scene partners. He kept pulling me back just slightly — enough to realize that I didn't have to project my feelings. He has encouraged me to just feel the emotions, and that being real will read, even in a big house. I sometimes wrestle between making what I'm saying as truthful as possible and making sure the Yiddish sounds perfectly authentic. Finding the balance of having the emotional intentions and being completely present, while having the Yiddish sound great is a goal that I strive for daily. I'm not always successful, but when I am successful, my performance feels more complete to me.

When I started working on "Now I Have Everything" I was thinking about how to make it sound as pretty as possible. I had a musical theatre background from Elon, but then I transferred to Juilliard and focused solely on classic technique. The more I worked with Joel Grey, the more I learned that I didn't have to be so musically strict with myself. It became more about spontaneity and endowing meaning to each word. When we were recording the cast album of *Fiddler*, Joel told me that what he wanted me to do in the song was "discover." The song is about the discovery of every moment, and how Perchik is saying everything for the first time. He is finding this love of Hodl that is as big as his ideals for being a leader and changing the world. Perchik is discovering his candidness in the song, and how he has grown from meeting Hodl and all of the people in Anatevka. I really enjoyed singing for the cast recording, and how everyone who had ever been in the cast came together to be a part of it. Making that album, being in the beautiful Manhattan Center, seeing everyone get to sing their songs, it all just felt overwhelmingly incredible, and such an honor to be a part of. I think that was the most exciting day of this whole process for me. Playing Perchik has also been so rewarding. This show is rich in lessons, and the arc of the story with the tragedies involved has been eye opening to me. Perchik really cares to work for the benefit of all people, and it has helped me see outside myself. Playing this role, I'm becoming more aware of how I fit in the puzzle of my community, and this world.

Part Five
Mishpokhe

Sammy

Role: Beylke

Back at the museum, we continued to stage and rehearse the show. We were scheduled to do a "stumble through" of Act One at the end of the week, which seemed like an impossible feat. There were many big scenes and numbers we hadn't yet touched, and it felt like we were spending all of our time rehearsing "Tradition."

One of my favorite things we blocked that week was "Sabbath Prayer." Stás, our choreographer, said we were going to try two ways of staging the number: first, a realistic approach that Joel Grey wanted to see, and second, the traditional Jerome Robbins setup. Stás gathered the immediate family and their Sabbath guests around a small table; the table was placed vertically, with the parents standing at the upstage head of the table, and the youngest daughters seated at the downstage head. It was a real, cozy family dinner table. Stás gave Golde and Tevye a few things to do with the candles, challah, and kiddush cup, and then we just sang through the number, all looking at each other around the little table. It was so intimate and simple, and we felt like a real family saying our Sabbath prayer. We were immediately overcome with emotion from the beauty of it all. Steven Skybell and Mary Illes, playing Tevye and Golde, could barely sing the beginning of the song through their tears. They looked into every one of our eyes and sang to us straight from their hearts. The daughters and I were all just sitting there, beaming up at our show parents with tears flowing freely. The Yiddish lyrics were so moving, and I could tell how present everyone at that table was. Glancing at the faces around me, I knew that it was going to feel natural to play a part of this family onstage. When the song ended, Stás started talking to us about trying the second staging option. I was still staring at Steven, completely mesmerized by him and his kind eyes, until Joel tapped me on the shoulder and said, "He's talking to you; you should pay attention. It could be useful." I of course turned red and quickly snapped my eyes to Stás. The second version of the staging, which we ended up sticking with for the show, used the table horizontally: the daughters lined up in age order, standing on the upstage side of the table, with the parents at the head. It was just as effective: the daughters were pressed almost shoulder to shoulder, and Tevye and Golde could look down the line of us, into each of our eyes. The daughters couldn't look at each other any more because of the setup, but it was amazing because we got to send all of our energy to our parents.

Staging the wedding scene was another remarkable accomplishment that we finally finished that week. The wedding scene starts with "Sunrise, Sunset," continues through "Wedding Dance One" which includes the two chairlifts and the bottle dance, then through a long scene, continues with "Wedding Dance Two," and ends with the pogrom. It is the Act One finale, it takes about twenty minutes, and it involves the entire cast being onstage for the majority of the time. There are a lot of intricate parts in the scene: there are always multiple dances happening, and people interacting with each other on the sides of the stage. Meanwhile, the main action in the scene involves an escalating argument between Tevye and Leyzer-Volf, which includes many fast-paced interjections from all different characters. We did several "Yiddish speed throughs"s of the scene, where everyone stood in a circle and spoke their lines in sequence as quickly as possible. This helped the fluidity and pace of the scene, and added an energy and urgency to the onstage interjections. We ran the dances over and over again, so Stás could make sure everyone had the moves down in a way that captured his intended style of the choreography. On top of this, there were set changes and prop moves that had to be taken care of. The whole thing took so long to block, that when Stás finally said, "Okay, let's do the entire scene from the top, and this time we will go through the pogrom too," the cast cheered with relief. Jackie Hoffman hilariously said to the room, "Wow. Never in the world has there been a group of Jews so excited for a pogrom." We all broke out in laughter.

At the end of the week, it was time for our first "stumble through" of Act One. We had a rehearsal in the morning, and it was a beautiful day outside so our whole cast sat in the grass and had a picnic for lunch. It was so fun, and we were all filled with excitement when we went back to the rehearsal room to run the act. The floor was marked with colorful tape to show the spacing and where the wings, set pieces, and boundaries were. On the side of the room, there was a table full of props, which I immediately went to peek at. We all put on our shmatas and rehearsal skirts, looked over our scripts one last time, and got ready to start. Then, Joel surprised me with the best gift a twenty-year-old playing a nine-year-old in a musical could have imagined — a doll. The doll was about as big as my hand, and had a cute, blue dress and tiny pigtails. He said it was mine to use throughout the entire show. I excitedly wrote a backstory for the doll and decided to name her "Baby Beylke." Our assistant stage manager, the amazing Rachel Calter, found a little piece of rope to tie around my waist so that I could have a place to put her when I wasn't holding onto her. Then Joel came over to untie the rope from around my waist and re-tied it around the doll to turn it into a sort of necklace for me. I suddenly had my very own personal prop, hanging around my neck, and I was overjoyed and already thinking of the many different ways I could use it. I'm still constantly playing around with how I can use Baby Beylke onstage, and some of my favorite moments have developed from it. Just recently, I decided to surprise Steven Skybell by holding the doll up in front of my face when he comes to kiss all of the daughters before "Sabbath Prayer." He laughed with shock and delight, and being the wonderfully adaptive and responsive actor that he is, gave Baby Beylke a big smooch on the forehead.

The "stumble through" was magical, imperfect, stressful, fun, nerve-wracking, and beautiful. It seemed like we had just started rehearsing, and suddenly we had half of a musical on its feet. To be able to experience the through-line of the whole first act was incredible. In addition to that, we were seeing our talented castmates do a lot of scenes and songs in the musical that we had never seen or heard fully before. When Steven performed "Rich Man" for the first time in front of everyone, the room was absolutely silent. Everyone was very familiar with that classic song, but what Steven brought to it was incomparable. I could not look away from that performance for one second; I still watch it from the wings almost every day. When he was finished, the whole cast erupted into a wholehearted round of applause. From that moment on, there was no doubt that we were in good hands. Our "stumble through" was a little rocky, but also filled with amazing, moving moments. By the time the pogrom ended, there wasn't a dry eye in the room. We had little time left before tech week, and still a long way to go, but we felt something real brewing in that rehearsal room.

* * *

Michael Einav

Role: Ensemble | Motl, Perchik, Der Rov Understudy

Since I'm an understudy in the show, I have had the privilege of working with many people in intimate scenes. I was fortunate enough to work with the amazing Steven Skybell as both Motl and as Perchik. It's so incredible because he is such a good actor. He is so powerful and such a giving scene partner. Whenever I'm on stage with him, I feel like a better actor in a lot of ways. When Steven looks you in the eye onstage, it just makes you feel like the character. I'm just so grateful. He is seriously one of a kind. He is so invested and he is so Tevye. I had scenes with him as both Motl and Perchik who are complete opposites in a lot of ways. When I'm on as Motl in the "Rebuttal" scene, I'm actually scared of him. I'm really just scared of him onstage, and I have to find the true courage in me to say what Motl has to say and fight for him. The interaction is so amazing.

There is something incredible about this cast. When an understudy goes on, it's so different from the actor who does it every night and sometimes it is hard to have a different scene partner, but everyone is really supportive. Rachel Zatcoff and Stephanie Lynne Mason were both so supportive and into it, and I had so much fun when I went on with them. It was really awesome and fun to work with Stephanie, as our characters play the games they play, flirt with each other, and fall in love. Doing "Miracle of Miracles" with Rachel was amazing. Her look, her spark, and her eyes are indescribably beautiful. She is such a good Tsaytl and in that scene she is so in love with Motl, so proud of him, and so happy that he finally stood up for the both of them. When I sing to her, her eyes just reflect all of that. She looks at me and gives me everything she's got, and I just see love. She is so good, it's amazing. I love both characters and all my scene partners so much.

Joel Grey cares so much about this show. He came to my first put in for Motl downtown because I was the first understudy to go on and he spent a lot of time with me. He's very demanding and I love it because he challenges me. I always want to make him happy and proud. He also knows how to get whatever it is that he wants to get out of you. I love working with him.

Backstage I have a tradition of dancing with our assistant stage manager Rachel Calter. During "Miracle of Miracles" we have a dance, and during the exodus scene we have a dance. We've been doing it since previews downtown and the dances just keep getting better. We keep adding to it too. I don't have any superstitious traditions, but I do always take a deep breath before we start the show. I take a breath and just think, *I do what I love.*

* * *

Nick Raynor

Role: Yosl | Ensemble | Fiddler, Fyedke Understudy

Being a part of *Fiddler* reminds me of how amazing it is to have a cast that feels like a family. We all want to be here doing the work, and everyone is so tight, caring, and loving. It is so nice to show up to work every day with those kinds of people, and I don't think I've ever experienced that before to this extent. Maybe we have our creative team or the show to thank for that. Usually as a dancer you get really close to the choreographer and never get to talk to the director. The way that Joel made sure to get to know his dancers was so awesome. I remember a couple days into the rehearsal, the dancer boys were all hanging out and Joel came over and started talking to us, and we were all shocked. He really made the first move to come over and get to know us. He continued to get to know us through the rehearsal and show process.

The assistant choreographer Merete Muenter has been my mentor for six years; she directed and choreographed me at Woodstock Playhouse. She got me my first national tour of *A Chorus Line,* and we've been in contact ever since. She texted me one day and said that I had to audition for this Yiddish production of *Fiddler on the Roof.* I was starting another contract at that time, so I asked her if I could send in a video submission. I didn't really know what the choreographer Staś would want to see, so I took a video that had me doing a lot of different tricks and dance moves. I kept getting emails back from Staś asking to see different things, so I kept sending more and more videos to audition with. I think I'm the only one who got hired from video submissions, so that was really cool. My first day of rehearsal was me meeting the entire creative team for the first time. It's always a blast with Merete, and it's been amazing working on *Fiddler* with her. I wouldn't be here without her.

The hardest thing I have to do in the show is jump off of a table in the song "To Life." When Staś Kmieć initially asked me to do it, the show was only supposed to run for six weeks. My body was not truly prepared to be doing it for over a year. It's kind of a blessing in disguise to face a challenge like that and be able to become this strong. I've never dropped the bottle during the bottle dance, but I did drop it once when the dance was over. I was dropping it into my hands, and all of a sudden my hands were so slippery that the bottle went right into the audience. I completely broke the fourth wall. It plopped onto a woman's lap and her face was just priceless. I wish I had a snapshot of that moment, because it was dangerously hysterical. We got the bottle back during intermission — thank goodness.

I've been working so hard for the past five years to become a member of the Actor's Equity Association. Last year I made it a goal to get my equity card. I was deciding between doing *Fiddler*, which was a non-union contract for me, and *A Chorus Line,* where I was going to be able to get points towards getting my equity card. *Fiddler* was only a six-week contract, but for some reason *Fiddler* just seemed so special. I wanted to work with Merete and Joel Grey, so I kind of decided to put my Equity dream on hold. Everything always works out as it should though, and *Fiddler* just kept extending. Eventually we moved uptown to Stage 42, and I got offered an Equity contract. It was such a huge milestone for me and I really didn't expect it to happen that way. I'm so grateful for all of it. On opening night at Stage 42, our Equity deputy Ben Liebert gave all of the new Equity members a little orientation. The new Equity members stood in the middle of the stage, surrounded by a circle of the rest of the whole cast, crew, and creative team. Ben read us Elia Kazan's poem, "The Actor's Vow" and I was just standing there sobbing. Being surrounded by all of that support and being read a beautiful poem with everyone cheering us on was very special. Ben was so amazing in making us feel welcome into the Equity family. I tried to soak up every second of that moment.

Part Six
Plotz

Sammy

Role: Beylke

The first thing I learned on the day of the Sitzprobe was what an "Equity cot" is. The Sitzprobe was in the big events hall upstairs, where we had occasionally rehearsed scenes with Joel. The big, round dinner tables were pushed aside; the room was a huge, open space, surrounded by windows. The creative team and crew sat at a long table in the front of the room, facing the band in the middle of the room. Behind the band, there were microphones in stands lined up for the singers, and behind the table on the other side were chairs for the cast to sit in when we weren't singing. In the corner, to my surprise, was a little bed. I turned to Rachel Zatcoff and asked, "What's with the weird little bed in the corner?"

She replied, "It's the Equity cot."

I asked, "What the heck is an Equity cot?" She explained. "It's a cot that they have to have backstage for anyone on an Equity contract. It's for if anyone needs to nap or wants to lay down or anything." I completely thought she was messing with me. Only after asking three more people about it did I decide to take her answer seriously.

When the Sitzprobe began, I was all aglow. Getting to finally sing with the whole orchestra was so fulfilling and fun. As soon as the band started playing "Tradition," the cast was grinning from ear to ear; the orchestra was pulsing spirit into the room with every note. Every song sounded beautiful, and it was such an exciting day. After the five of us daughters sang "Matchmaker," we ran together for a big group hug, just like we do at the end of the song onstage. When the boys sang "To Life" we all joyfully danced around in the back of the room, and Raquel and I lip-synced to Cameron Johnson's long-held note. I watched Zalmen Mlotek gleefully conduct, and thought, *there is no place I would rather be.*

The next day we had a full run through of the show in the same room. The creative team, the crew, and all of the costume, set, lighting, wig, and sound designers were there watching the run. It was extremely nerve-wracking. I expertly tied my rehearsal shmata and slid into my skirt, and then we performed the whole show. We were so exhausted that when we got our ten-minute break, Rachel flung herself on the floor next to the sign-in sheet. I ran over and lay down next to her — one of many times we collapsed to lay on the ground, side by side, during the tough rehearsal process.

The following day, July 1st, 2018, marked the start of tech week. Before all of the elements of costumes, microphones, lights, hair, and makeup were worked into the show, we had our first full spacing rehearsal on the stage. We started from the top of the show, and ran the scenes to see how they fit on the stage, while making any needed adjustments. The theatre was beautiful, if not for lack of wing space. Props hung on the walls and shelves in the long hallway behind the stage, and chairs and tables crowded the sides. After "Tradition" ended, I stood in the tiny wing on stage right with Stephanie and Rachel, waiting to enter for the first scene. Stephanie was supposed to enter first with a basket of laundry, and then I would run out halfway through her line, with Rachel running on afterwards to catch up with me. We all looked at each other excitedly, thinking, *this is happening. We are doing this show for real.* I jumped up and down in the wing, listening to the first couple line exchanges with Golde, Shprintze, and Khave, and waiting for Stephanie to go on stage. Suddenly, I couldn't hear the lines any more. Stephanie turned around to Rachel and me and said, "Oh god." I tried to peek around her to see what was going on, and then Rachel asked, "Did he just stop them?" Stephanie nodded, and sure enough, we could hear the entire scene start again from the beginning. What none of us expected at all during the spacing rehearsal was for Joel to stop us in the middle of the scene, which he did repeatedly. It was suddenly like the first rehearsal all over again: Joel was stopping the scene after almost every single line to work on the acting. It was a while before I actually got to go onstage, even though I have one of the first five lines in the scene. The first time we got to Stephanie's line, I ran out on the stage excitedly, seeing the huge empty house and feeling the adrenaline and anticipation of starting to say my first line. Before I could utter a word, Joel stopped Stephanie with a question about her line, so I turned around and ran right back off. It was pretty exhilarating, though slightly anticlimactic for me. Every time we restarted, or went back a couple of lines, I heard everyone laughing or groaning in frustration. I was bouncing on my tiptoes, waiting from the wings to run on and say my first line, and secretly having the time of my life. When I finally got to say my line, delighting in the victory, Joel calmly stopped me and said, simply, "This is very important! Go again." I ran back offstage and re-entered with even more urgency: asking where Tate was as if it were a life or death situation. To this day I still jump around in the wings before I run on for the opening scene, reminding myself to keep the same urgency and passion from that first day of rehearsal on the stage.

During Tech Week, our rehearsal room was transformed: a big wall went up in the middle, dividing the room into the women's and men's dressing rooms. Golde and Yente shared a little room surrounding a bathroom backstage, and Tevye and Leyzer-Volf shared a different small closet-like space outside of the bathroom in the rehearsal room on the men's side. The rest of the cast found their name tags along a set of tables with mirrors on top of them in the two halves of the room. Though it was by no means the lovely dressing room I had imagined I would be in for my fancy, Off-Broadway debut, I was delighted to find my name hanging on the right-hand side end table. It was a tiny table that I shared with Raquel, perfect for our two little selves. Directly behind us sat Rachel, Stephanie, Rosie, and Kayleen Seidl, who is an amazing ensemble member that covers all three of the older daughters. The four of them were faced away from us, towards the inside of the room, on a huge table with a double-sided mirror running down the center. On the other side of the mirror sat the rest of the women. I giddily settled at my little dressing room station, waving at Rachel through the reflection. There was a little Rice Krispie treat on each of our seats that said "Happy Tech! Love, Stage Management," written on the wrapper in Sharpie. I joyfully ate mine, and anyone else's who didn't want theirs because Rice Krispie treats are my absolute favorite. When everyone arrived, we got into our microphones and costumes for the first time. Ann Hould-Ward, our costume designer, had magnificent costumes for us that we had previously been fitted for. We couldn't wait to snatch the gorgeous skirts, blouses, and costume pieces from the hangers, and finally see the whole cast transform into their characters. We gushed over each other's outfits and spun around in our dresses and skirts to see how beautifully they floated up. There were endless photos and giggles — it felt like a family fashion show. I discreetly watched the older girls do their makeup and tried to follow suit. Then Raquel and I braided our hair and tied each other's shmatas, making sure our microphones poked out just the right amount with the help of Jordan Porch, one of our wonderful audio technicians. Before we knew it, we were onstage in full "tech mode."

With only three days of tech rehearsal before our first preview for an audience, emotions and energy of all types were running high. In the midst of the chaos, Raquel and I were being tossed in and out of "Matchmaker." "Matchmaker" had been a crazy kerfuffle from the beginning: Staś and Joel had different visions for the number, and both of them didn't really know exactly what to do with the two of us younger daughters, since we don't have any solo lines in the song. We started off with broomsticks, doing light sweeping in the beginning of the number until Rachel snatched the brooms to demonstrate the suitors to the other sisters. Every time we ran the number, Joel and Staś would tell us we were sweeping too much, not enough, unrealistically, too loudly, too nonchalantly, or just not the right way. There seemed to be no doing it right, and eventually the brooms got cut from the number because the whole thing was too "schticky" for Joel's taste anyway. Once the brooms were cut, they decided to try the number without the two of us younger daughters. Joel put Rachel on her knees to imitate Yente's stature, which ended up being hilarious, and then Staś brought laundry into the song to play with instead. With the new additions, they added Beylke and Shprintze back into the number; we happily folded laundry and listened to the older sisters talk until it was time to sing with them. Every time we ran it, though, there was something about what we were doing in the number, or maybe just our presence in the song, that was off-putting to Joel. We weren't getting any specific notes about what we could do in the song to make it work, but Staś and Joel kept pulling us in and out of the number. Raquel and I had many discussions about what we could do to get them to keep us in the number, but nothing we tried kept them from cutting us from the song again and again.

During that first staging rehearsal, we got to be in the number, but when we got offstage, we were informed that we were going to be cut from it again for the time being. Our stage manager, Kat, told all of the daughters to just check the callboard every morning during tech week to find out which version of "Matchmaker" we would be doing — the version with Beylke and Shprintze, or the version without. I was extremely upset about being cut because "Matchmaker" was one of my favorite numbers to be a part of, and it was really special getting to do that number with all five of the daughters. Raquel and I held our heads high, though, and crossed our fingers that they would put us back in the number the next day. Later in the day, we got to the end of the show and ran the song "Anatevka," which the two of us were also quietly a part of. When we got to the end of the song, Kat called a ten-minute break for everyone, asking Raquel and me to stay behind for a minute. We walked to the end of the stage to meet Kat, Staś, and Joel, and they told us that we were cut from "Anatevka." We went back to the dressing room, trying to be positive and not let it get to us. As soon as someone asked us what happened and we had to announce that we were cut from yet another number, I started tearing. Luckily, the room instantly overflowed with loving support, so my tears didn't stand a chance. Everyone started sharing their frustrations and woes, relating to us and offering comfort, and Kayleen even gave me a piece of what she refers to as "emergency chocolate." I couldn't help but feel all warm and fuzzy inside, and by the time we were called back to rehearsal, it didn't seem to matter what numbers I was or wasn't in. I was in *Fiddler on the Roof in Yiddish*, and I was a part of a beautiful, special family. The next day, Raquel and I were put back in "Matchmaker," and we haven't wavered since.

* * *

Merete Muenter

Assistant Choreographer

From a dancer/choreographer perspective, learning Jerome Robbins' original choreography for *Fiddler* was incredibly valuable, not only because of the dance elements, but because of how clearly the choreography is used for storytelling. It's a master class for teaching a choreographer what movements are important to convey a story on stage, and the structure of how to highlight different people and areas on the stage so the audience knows where to look. I also learned about the in-depth research Robbins did to make *Fiddler* historically and culturally accurate during his creative process. Robbins' choreography for *West Side Story* wove the movement into the action so seamlessly that you almost didn't realize they were dancing. It just made sense that they were dancing, and the movement became such a natural part of the fabric of the whole production that the audience never questioned it. Robbins utilized that same approach again so well in *Fiddler*. Within his work, he created these beautiful pictures with the people on stage whether they were moving or standing still. Those pictures allow the audience to absorb what is happening and get to know the characters and see their relationships within the shtetl. It also gives the performers the ability to come together as a unified whole within the context of Anatevka.

Regarding Jerome Robbins as an innovator, one of the best examples of this is his "bottle dance" during the wedding scene, which is now considered one of his most classic pieces of choreography. This dance is a great example of how important stillness is in choreography as well as movement. As I did my own research during the rehearsal process for *Fiddler* in Yiddish, I was surprised to learn that bottle dances aren't an actual tradition at Jewish weddings. It was Jerome Robbins' research and ideas that led to its creation. Now it has become such a staple at Jewish weddings that people don't realize it originated from Robbins' work in *Fiddler.* The bottle dance is one of my favorite moments in the show, as is the dance it leads into called "whips and hooks." I love the combination of athleticism and discipline for that style of choreography. There is such a sharp contrast of performing the slow controlled movements of the bottle dance into the frenetic style of "whips and hooks," which gives the audience a sense of excitement and unpredictability. The rehearsal process for the bottle dance was challenging and repetitive. It's very militant in terms of its structure and precision, and the exact footwork, body placement, and balance elements have to be drilled over and over again so it can be performed the same way every time using muscle memory. It is beautiful because it is simple and complicated at the same time, and it requires strict attention to detail. One of my favorite things about being involved in *Fiddler* has been watching the progress of the cast and how they now own their work in the show. I love to look back on old pictures and rehearsal videos of the guys dropping bottles all over the floor. Now I see how polished they are, and I sometimes forget that they made a lot of mistakes back when they were learning it.

One number that went through several incarnations was "Matchmaker." This number was one of the parts of the show that took the longest to stage, because Joel felt it was missing something in the storytelling and he wanted to get it right. I remember his work sessions with the daughters, which became a trial and error process of finding the truth in the lyrics and who these young girls are as they are about to grow into women. He didn't want the number to turn into staged business about sweeping the floors or folding laundry. "Matchmaker" is much more important than that, because it is the one time when the audience is introduced to these girls, who they are, what their hopes and dreams are, and what the relationships are between them. After this, the audience never sees all five of them alone in a room again. It's imperative for the audience to fall in love with the daughters during "Matchmaker," because we still have to love them when they grow up and start to have opinions of their own that don't follow Tevye's ideas of tradition. Tevye's story about tradition and fatherhood can't be told until we know who his daughters are first: once we know who they are, the story can build on the challenges and heartbreak Tevye faces as he says goodbye to Tsaytl, Hodl and Khave. "Matchmaker" sets the stage for all of that and starts to move the story forward. Since our production is being done in Yiddish, the staging becomes even more vital. If the audience watches "Matchmaker" without the benefit of English supertitles, the staging/movement still has to inform the audience what is going on regardless of what language is being spoken. For all those reasons, "Matchmaker" remained a work in progress for several weeks until Joel was satisfied that the story about the daughters was coming through clearly.

I have many fond memories of this *Fiddler* experience, but I think my favorite moments are when I was able to watch Joel rehearse with the cast. He knew the show very well already, but his understanding of the show grew even more as he became more acclimated to the Yiddish. The Yiddish established further understanding of the time period, storyline and relationships for everybody, because it added this layer of authenticity that was even more relevant than anybody expected. I also really appreciated how Joel kept every character completely based in truth. Joel is a director who knows how to "keep it real," and I learned a lot by watching him work with that foundation of reality. The moment I appreciate the most in our show is the tearing of the Torah page at the end of the pogrom. It succeeds in slapping the audience into the reality of the situation, because it's so violating and shocking. It was something Joel put into the show that isn't in the script, and I admire him for taking that risk.

The initial rehearsal process was probably the most emotional rehearsal process I have ever been involved in. The actors were connecting to the material in such an intense and personal way, and it was thrilling to have an opportunity to take risks in order to breathe new life into a classic piece of theatre while maintaining the integrity of such an important story. Watching the show blossom under Joel's love and guidance, and watching the relationships grow between everybody in the cast and with Joel was heartwarming. We are here for all the right reasons. *Fiddler* is about keeping the love alive and moving forward with acceptance, while always remembering where you came from. It has created a family for us where we all grow together onstage and off. This unique experience happens once in a lifetime if you are lucky, and we will all look back on this and remember how fortunate we were, and still are, to be a part of it.

* * *

Kayleen Seidl

Role: Ensemble | Tsaytl, Hodl, Khave Understudy

I've never understudied multiple roles at once before this. It is an interesting challenge, especially in a different language. Before rehearsals started, I didn't know exactly what my ensemble lines would be or what vocal part they would put me on, so I really took the opportunity to get a head start on the daughters' tracks. Their parts are laid out in the script, so I focused on learning those lines. I started with Khave because she says the least, so that was the easiest to get under my belt. As soon as I got the script, I got colored highlighters, colored pencils, and colored tabs. I assigned a color to each girl so I could easily focus on one daughter at a time when flipping through the script. When the girls are all in the same number, I can see which blocking is for which girl which is super helpful. It's a lot to keep track of, especially in numbers that I'm in myself because I'm understudying and in the ensemble of the show. Now that I know my tracks and we're up and running, I pick a show each week to shadow each daughter so that I can really learn their track from start to finish. I also try to pick two or three adjectives that fit each girl for me so that there's a mindset I can put myself into quickly when switching between the three. If I have to jump in quickly to that character, that's a tool that I find really helpful. There are always new things that pop up in my mind character-wise. For example, doing my Khave put-in with the cast, I realized that her personality is probably the most foreign to me because she's the youngest of the three and I don't tend to feel the youngest ever.

The first time I went on for one of my understudy-tracks it was exciting, and it was nice because it was a planned date. I knew I was going to go on and happened to get a put-in that day, which was really helpful. It was a little scary too though. As Tsaytl, I ran out right after Beylke for the first scene. I kind of got out there and thought, *Oh shit. Here we are. What's my first line?* But it came to me and it was good. Funnily enough, I don't really remember any audience reactions, which I guess is good because I was so in it. When you get really comfortable in a role, you sometimes notice audience feedback. You start to think, *Are they laughing there? Did anything weird happen?* and that sort of thing. I don't remember any of that. So my biggest takeaway was being able to stay focused and in it, which is really important in any show.

I had booked the role of Christine in Yeston's *Phantom* at the Westchester Broadway Theatre before we started *Fiddler*, and at the time they didn't conflict. *Phantom* was supposed to start after we finished our run of *Fiddler*, but then we kept extending. I had to decide if it was still worth doing, since I would have to leave *Fiddler* to do it. Ultimately, I decided that Christine was a great role for me; and since it was at a regional house that was so close to the city, it just felt right. There was definitely a part of me that was thinking, *what if they make a cast album, and what if we transfer, and what if I miss out on all of these things?* It worked out perfectly though. I had a break during the *Phantom* run and was able to come back and do the original cast recording in the middle of that. Then I had one day between *Phantom* ending and coming back to *Fiddler* rehearsals for the transfer. Coming back into the show, there was a part of me that was a little nervous that I wouldn't remember everything and would have to relearn it. Luckily a lot was still there. Having drilled the lines so much, again especially in another language, once they're in there they're really so in there. It was a whirlwind, but I honestly just got blessed that it all worked out the way it did. I loved getting to do *Phantom*, but I'm really happy to be back with this group. It's such a meaningful story we're telling. It's so pertinent and it's making such an impact on the audiences who are seeing it, and that's really special to be a part of in any capacity.

* * *

James Števko

Role: Mendl | Ensemble

On our first day of rehearsal downtown, they decided to do a sing-through of "Tradition." I was sitting in a chair next to Josh Dunn, and we both weren't available for the optional Yiddish coaching the week before, so we were really sweating in our seats. I didn't stop sweating until we got through the entire book read. The most nerve-wracking moment of my life was probably sitting in that chair and waiting for my lines. I was speaking them in front of everyone before I had spoken them in front of anyone. I'm quite confident in the fact that we all felt like that the first day.

I had always assumed the bottle dance was some kind of trick. Turns out, it wasn't. It's a real bottle on a real hat. It was very nerve-wracking... but the bottle smells fear. I figured out that it is mostly about placing the bottle on the hat and maintaining stillness and calmness. The biggest factor is actually that the hat has to be on correctly before you put the bottle on it. It's the preparation that really counts. In rehearsal, the choreographer Staś Kmieć had us all doing jetes across the floor with bottles on our heads. You have to be comfortable with the bottle wobbling or bouncing up and down. That's where the calmness comes in, and that was the biggest help in learning how to master the bottle dance. When I feel myself getting nervous, I talk myself into boredom. It's an approach used by Olympic athletes. I'll move my joints to warm up, but I try not to stretch. When my muscles are loose and relaxed, it actually makes all of the knee work so much more exhausting. I need to go in a little stronger than I do for anything else.

I will never forget opening night and making my Off-Broadway debut. Specifically, I will always remember the bottle dance in the wedding scene. You could feel the excitement of the opening night audience. Going down to our knees when the music was building, and then doing the first knee slide with the cymbals crashing behind us was magical. There was excitement in the air and the cast was clapping and the cymbals were all crashing. That is one of my favorite moments. Aside from that, the biggest night for me was when Hal Prince came to see the show. Joel introduced him to the entire audience. It was one of those mind-blowing, legendary Broadway moments. Hal produced the original *Fiddler on the Roof* while Joel was originating his role in *Cabaret*. All of that history in that tiny theatre just blew me away. It's something I never would have dreamed of.

Part Seven
Simkhe

Sammy

Role: Beylke

On the night of the first preview of *Fiddler*, Rachel had all of the girls in the dressing room pick a "power thought card" from a deck she had of Louise Hay's power thought cards. We went around the room fifteen minutes before places were called and everyone read their cards, which was joyful and moving for us all. My card said: "My future is glorious."

When Kat, our stage manager, called places for the top of the show, we all lined up backstage for "Tradition." We stood hand in hand down the backstage crossover: a long, slightly rounded hallway behind the stage that connected the stage right and stage left wings. We passed hand-squeezes around and whispered excitedly, and then suddenly fell silent as the pre-show announcements began. The next minute, I heard the violin playing and got goosebumps all down my arms. Steven began saying his opening lines, the orchestra came in, and we all started to hold on to each other's hands tighter. I took a deep breath, and then the drums came in and we started pulsing our arms and stomping onto the stage. I thought my cheeks would fall off from not being able to contain my ridiculously big smile during the entirety of "Tradition." When the opening number was over, I ran offstage, grabbed my doll, and got ready to run on for the first scene. I was bouncing up and down with my doll when Steven said his last line of the song — that's when we heard the thunderous applause. It was the loudest applause I had ever heard. Everyone who was backstage took a second to look at each other with jaw-dropping awe and excitement before the scene change began. When the scene change started, I stood in the wing completely alone. I put one hand on my heart and one hand on my abdomen and thought of a phrase that my teacher Randy Graff taught me: "Nothing to prove, only to share." Then I started jumping up and down, and when Stephanie and Rachel came back from moving a table in the scene change, we exchanged quick, but very full smiles. I jumped around in the wings until my cue line, and then bolted onto the stage — the rest was a blur.

The applause after "Tradition" was nothing in comparison to the applause we received at the end of the show. There wasn't a dry eye on the stage or in the audience, and it felt like we had just done something truly remarkable. We celebrated with our guests and the audience at a party in the events hall, watching barely visible fireworks through the big open windows for the Fourth of July. I took pictures pointing at my name on the sign that lists all of the cast, stuffed my face with chocolate babka, and basically wandered around the party like a lost toddler until it was time to go home.

We had done our first preview for an audience, but we still had a little way to go before opening night. That week, we had rehearsal every morning and a preview every night, or vice versa. It was just as exhausting as it sounds. During rehearsal, Ben Liebert brought in "Bananagrams," the word game, and we all played frequently. I was one of the constant reigning champions, alongside Ben. Through the week we got a lot of notes and worked on scenes and some changes based on the feel of the show with an audience. During one of our first rehearsals, Joel came up to me and thoughtfully said, "I think we should get you some glasses." He then took his own glasses off of his face, said, "Here, try this on," and gently slid them into place behind my ears. It was adorable and bizarre. The next day I had a new pair of glasses at my dressing room station from the wardrobe team. Everyone thought they were super cute on me; I felt like I couldn't see clearly and looked like a tiny grandma with a big, squishy nose. It took a few weeks for me to warm up to them, but I finally decided that I didn't look like a tiny grandma and that they were pretty cute. I still can't say they are my favorite accessory, but when I make someone laugh by having to push them up my nose onstage, it's well worth it.

After what felt like the longest week, we made it to

July 15th, 2018, which was opening night. It seemed like a magical night; the dressing rooms were filled with flower deliveries, candy, and other gifts. Merete, our assistant choreographer made us all little rubber ducks that resembled our characters; we all wrote cards for each other, and we were gifted beautiful bracelets with violins on them from the team at the National Yiddish Theatre Folksbiene. Our dressing rooms were practically overflowing with joyful gifts. Rachel's station was glowing with sunflowers, and even Raquel's curls were bouncier than usual. For me, it was my official Off-Broadway debut and I was over the moon. We pulled power thought cards again in the girl's room, and Joel came in and picked a card that said: "My income is constantly increasing." We all laughed hysterically, and when he left, we started gushing about our opening night excitement. All of the girls in the dressing room ended up in a sort of huddle, which quickly turned into a big group hug. I cried happy tears and jumped around the room in excitement until we got our "five minutes until places" call. Since it was our first real show, I wasn't the only one who went backstage early. As I was heading out of the dressing to go backstage, I felt something in my shoe. It felt like a rock or tiny piece of a pretzel, but when I unzipped my boot and shook it upside-down, a huge, beautiful spider fell out and started crawling around. It was a frightening and shocking way to start the show, but I was told it meant good luck and other good things. I went around to the stage right wing to make sure my doll was set for me to easily grab between "Tradition" and the first scene, and then I ran into Rachel who was doing vocal warmups. We excitedly greeted the musicians as they got ready to play the show, and then headed back to stage left where everyone was buzzing around. I was grinning from ear to ear, and when Jackie Hoffman heard people talking about how it was my Off-Broadway debut, she made up a little verse for me to the tune of "The Dream." She sang, "Your Off-Broadway debut — mazel tov, mazel tov! An Anatevka Jew — mazel tov, mazel tov!" Everyone around us laughed and cheered, while I beamed and blushed.

When we entered the stage for "Tradition," the audience, to our surprise and delight, roared with applause. The energy coming from our opening night audience was breathtaking. They cheered us on from that very first entrance through our very last bow. Our energy was just as maximized, though by intermission I was so exhausted that I plopped down on the equity cot and closed my eyes for a minute. Joel came on stage to make opening night remarks during our curtain call, and we all gushed as he talked about what a special group of people we are. He talked about his history with Yiddish too, and then sang the song his father wrote for him as a young performer in the Borscht Belt, "When I Was Eight Days Old."

After the show, we all flocked to the dressing rooms and changed into our fancy opening night dresses.

Everyone got ready for the party together, leaving the dressing room in little groups of whoever was dressed and ready first. The five sisters were the last to leave the dressing room, popping a mini champagne bottle for ceremonial purposes, and walking down the hallway to the party together. Rosalind Harris, who played Tzeitel in the original *Fiddler on the Roof* film, was there, and she talked to us about the show and what an amazing thing it is. The five sisters knelt on the ground in a circle around her, and I hung on her every word. Then she pulled out gifts for us: five sparkly pens to tell us that we all sparkle on stage. We took pictures, heard speeches, and squeezed our family and friends that were there. It was a beautiful, celebratory night for our special show. When I went home it was very late, but I stayed up reading opening night cards from everyone. I saved every single card in a special box, except for two that I framed because they made me cry. One was a beautiful note from Rachel, and the other was from Joel Grey himself, who simply said: "Darling, precious, and talented Samantha — you are a delight on stage. Wishing you everything good!"

* * *

Adam B. Shaprio

Role: Der Rov | Tevye, Leyzer-Volf, Avrom Understudy

It wasn't until standing backstage at our first preview that it suddenly occurred to me that we had to stand up to every other production of *Fiddler* that our audience had ever seen. We had been working so hard for three weeks and we were tunnel focused with the singing, acting, dancing, and Yiddish. The next thing I know I'm walking onto the stage and it's time to do the show. We go on and do the opening number, "Tradition." Then Tevye says his last line and we make our exit, and after the last chord of the song plays, we hear the audience cheering. It stopped me in my tracks. The scream that came from the audience was incredible; I have done performances where we don't get that kind of applause at the end of the show. I remember everyone that was offstage just sort of stopped and looked at each other. I could tell we were all thinking the same thing: *we may have something very special here.*

Working with Joel Grey was so exciting. My favorite moment with Joel was back when we had been in rehearsal for about a week. They were running the wedding dance, and I'm the only person not onstage for that. At this point it still did not feel normal to me to be in a room with the legendary Joel Grey. I was sitting to the side in a chair over by the coffee machine, and he came over and perched himself on my lap. He didn't look at me or say anything; he was just watching the rehearsal from my lap. I was freaking out and thinking, *this is a Tony Award and Oscar Award winning tuchas on my lap right now.* It was a head-explosion moment. Two days later he did it again after a vocal rehearsal and it turned into a whole Chicago bit. Everyone saw it and was laughing, and I have an awesome picture to remember it by.

As a cast we have gotten to celebrate a lot together, and I have made many cakes for many events. The first cake I made was about a week into the rehearsal process for our musical director Zalmen Mlotek's birthday. I've known Zalmen for almost eleven years, and I wanted to do something special for him. I did a cake for our original closing date downtown before the extension, and I did a cake for our first hundredth show. I made a cake for Jackie Hoffman's birthday, which was very fun and I wish someone had been filming her reaction of it. I also made a cake for Abby Goldfarb's surprise bridal shower. Then uptown I made Joel's birthday cake, which was awesome. I made pies for one understudy-put-in rehearsal, because I needed a break from cakes. Recently I made a cake for our hundredth show at Stage 42. I love making the cakes; it's something I do, and it's a great way to celebrate special occasions. Celebrating Hanukkah during the run of *Fiddler* downtown at the National Yiddish Theatre Folksbiene was really fun. For me, Hanukkah is a really happy time about being with your family, sharing memories, and lighting candles together. To be able to do that in the dressing room with our *Fiddler* family was so amazing. Only about half of us are actually Jewish, but it was such a great way to come together and celebrate the happy memories we have with each other since we all feel like family here. We also did a "Secret Shadkhnte" which was our version of "Secret Santa." Everyone who wanted to be a part of it signed up and drew names. There was a spending limit, but the fun part was that you could decide how you wanted to deliver your gifts before the big reveal. I had Rachel Zatcoff and I decided to do a series of small gifts accompanied by a series of printed notes with pop culture clue cards to my identity. Every night, when all of the girls had left the dressing room, I would slip in and leave something on her station. On the reveal date we had a little party on the stage, and everyone guessed who their "Shadkntes" were. People got really creative. Jodi Snyder wrote Jennifer Babiak a parody of "I Feel Pretty" called "Jen is Pretty" and got Rachel to deliver it as a singing telegram which was really cute. This cast is pretty amazing like that.

* * *

Lisa Fishman

Role: Bobe Tsaytl | Golde, Yente Understudy

I entered the show downtown in the summer as the Bobe Tsaytl replacement and Golde understudy. There wasn't time for them to rehearse everyone initially because they were already into production, so I had not yet received any rehearsal for understudying Golde. However, there were no dates that Jennifer Babiak, our Golde, was planning on going out, so it was okay. Meanwhile, I was learning the lines, watching and writing down all the blocking and choreography, and studying the costumes and props. I hadn't worked on it with anyone; I was just practicing, mostly alone in my living room. Suddenly one evening I was told by our stage manager that I was "on warn" for the next morning for Golde because Jen wasn't feeling well. Thankfully, I felt that I had everything down even though I hadn't been through it with anyone else. That night I drilled it over and over. Earlier, I had made recordings on my phone of the Golde scenes with me saying the other characters' lines, and with little moments of silence between so that I could practice. That night I probably went over each of those scene recordings three or four times. I rehearsed the choreography in my living room, and I was up until two in the morning making flowcharts of my entrances, costume changes, props, and other backstage logistics. I ended up with too many flowchart papers and I realized it was too big for the wall, so then I took a picture of everything and printed that out so it was all on one page. Then I made a smaller flowchart for the wings for all the quick changes and entrances that I wouldn't have time to run to the dressing room to check.

I had never once run into Jen on the way to the show, but that morning I ran into her for the first time as I was getting off the subway. She said that she was feeling okay, and she didn't want to put pressure on me because she knew I hadn't gotten a chance to run anything. I told her not to worry, that I was glad she could do the show, but also that I was ready to go on if she needed it. She did the show that afternoon, but by intermission I was given the heads up that she would probably have to call out that night. Jen was very kind to stay for a little while after the first show to talk through the props with me: where they "live," and how to work with them. We had a dinner break between shows, and then I was brought back and given thirty minutes with Tevye and then thirty minutes with the whole cast. With Tevye we just went onstage and hit whatever we considered the most important scenes to do in space and time. Then, the cast was brought in, and we did all the big group traffic and choreography numbers like "Tradition" and "The Wedding." That was all we had time for, and then it was time to get ready.

I was in laser focus mode. I couldn't believe that I

wasn't completely flipping out. Some wonderful force of confidence came over me. I had thirty minutes to get dressed and ready for the show and to get it all together. I remember Rachel Zatcoff saying to me: "Just do it in chunks." That was really helpful because there are breaks between scenes where I could go back and look at what was coming next. Somehow the whole thing ran incredibly smoothly. I still don't know how it happened, but it was magical. The cast is so supportive and loving and truly an amazing ensemble of real friendships. I had been going through some difficult experiences at the beginning of the uptown transfer, but the love and support I received from the whole cast and crew really helped to keep me afloat. Everyone has each other's backs. I so look forward to coming to the theatre every day and seeing everyone, including the orchestra and the crew. It is just a wonderful group of people, and I feel really blessed to be a part of it. It gives me such a sense of family. Just a few weeks ago, Stephanie Lynne Mason who plays Hodl had everyone over to watch "Game of Thrones." I don't even watch "Game of Thrones," but I just loved getting to be with everyone. There were probably forty people stuffed in her apartment, and she cooked and baked and made homemade popsicles. It was so amazing, and I just always have so much fun with this wonderful group of people.

Part Eight
L'Chaim

Sammy

Role: Beylke

The summer of performing *Fiddler* at the National Yiddish Theatre Folksbiene was one big, happy memory. Those three months felt so full of life and love. We truly formed a family, on and offstage, with friendships of all sorts that I know will last forever. It was a summer of getting to the theatre early and eating breakfast sandwiches from the deli around the corner, while reading Mary Oliver poetry by Rachel's recommendation. It was also a summer of wearing my overalls too many days in a row, in which, with dirty hair, I sometimes met esteemed people who attended the show. It was shimmering bursts of dreams and wonder in a deeply rooted, familial, heartful, messy everyday life.

Most days we started the show by pulling power thought cards, which was such a gift in itself. Sometimes we put on music and had amazing dance parties and singalongs before the show too. I held Stephanie's hair while she tied her shmata, and then I always tied Rosie's apron for her. Raquel and I did our makeup together, took silly selfies and videos, and talked about the Pure Barre classes we had taken that morning. There were always tons of snacks and goodies in the dressing room, and on special occasions Stephanie or Adam Shapiro would bake delicious treats for everyone to eat. Rachel and I greeted the orchestra before every show, and we went back and forth with them making jokes and guessing what famous people might be in the audience. Jordan Porch checked my microphone placement, and Tim Peters made sure my dress straps weren't too twisted. I held hands with Jodi and Bobby Underwood for "Tradition," and before the number started, Bobby always tried to tickle me — he was usually pretty successful. I took a minute to say, "Nothing to prove, only to share," as Randy Graff taught me, and spent a few seconds looking up at the high ceiling as Rachel taught me. Ben Liebert and I squeezed each other's hands to the beat during the vignettes in "Tradition," and then we laughed at Michael Einav's repeated shoe squeaking as we exited the number. Raquel and I danced with our assistant stage manager, Rachel Calter, to the beginning of "Matchmaker," before we entered every day, and when I exited, Rachel Calter always had her hand open to high-five me. After I gave her a high- five, I stopped at the edge of the wings to high-five each of the other daughters as they came offstage from the song. I watched Steven sing "If I Were a Rich Man," and I watched Rachel, Steven, and Ben in

113

the first "Rebuttal" scene from the wings: both never failed to completely mesmerize me. Before "Sabbath Prayer," I paid a visit to Jennifer Babiak and Jackie Hoffman in their little dressing room behind the stage, telling them any funny stories from the girls' dressing room that they hadn't heard yet. Raquel and I timed Cameron Johnson's long-held note in "To Life," and then announced his daily record to the room, the longest of which I remember being a whopping sixteen seconds. Rachel was the only one in the girls' dressing room not in "The Dream," so after watching her "Rebuttal" scene from the wings, I left her a little note on her station for her to find when she came back to the empty dressing room to change. Then I switched out my glasses for my "dream mask," and shuffled back to the wings to watch Ben and Rachel in the beautiful end of "Miracle of Miracles." I always took a moment while watching the end of that song to think of one thing I was grateful for in that moment. Kirk Geritano and I danced around before we ran on stage to move set pieces in the transition into "The Dream," and then Bobby Underwood and I danced around before we ran on stage to move set pieces in the transition out of "The Dream." After the transition, I picked up candles from the stage right wing to hand to all of the girls as they came backstage to get ready for the wedding scene. Rachel and I shared a quick chat on two chairs in the backstage crossover before everyone started coming down the hallway for the wedding, and then Raquel and I practiced our drumming skills on Mikhl Yashinsky's arm with our candles before we entered the scene, which was the last scene in Act One.

Snuggling on the equity cot was one of my favorite intermission pastimes; I usually shared it with Lauren Thomas or Kayleen. I also hung out in the boys' dressing room sometimes, read a book in the hallway, or just lay on the ground in the hallway with whomever was there. We played games, told stories, told riddles, stretched, snacked, chatted, and everything in between. The first thing I was in during Act Two was the "Tailor Shop Two" scene, but before that happened, I got to listen to my favorite song in the musical, "Do You Love Me." Our production's version of the song was the most special and beautiful thing ever, and my favorite part of the show. One day I followed Rachel backstage to hear the song from closer up, and she let me sit in her little spot with her where she listened to it before her entrance for "The Rumor." It became my most cherished tradition — Rachel sitting on a milk jug in a tiny crevice in the crossover, me kneeling on the ground next to her, leaning on her lap, and listening to "Do You Love Me."

I always tried to sing along to "The Rumor," backstage, because I thought it was the funniest thing ever, and then Raquel and I quickly came up with jokes or pranks to pull on Stephanie and Rachel before the "Khave Ballet Sequence." We jumped out to scare them, pretended like we were fighting, made bridges with our arms for them to cross under, jumped in circles around them, pretended like there was something wrong with their hair, and all sorts of crazy, little-sister things. Then we did weird, interpretive dance moves in the wings before dancing onto the stage. Before the last scene, Ben, Raquel, and I got our little bundles for the "Exodus" and sat together on the staircase next to the backstage area. At the end of the day, I took the train home from Battery Park with Jodi, Evan Mayer, Kirk, and anyone else who was going way uptown. Jodi went around and asked us all what snacks we were going to have when we got home, and if the subway car was empty, Evan and Jodi would put their water bottles on their heads and try to do the bottle dance on the moving train.

When we had matinee shows and the rest of the day off, the whole cast would often go out for food and drinks. After spending so much time at the theatre together, we still weren't sick of each other. I actually tried avocado for the first time at a Mexican restaurant that summer in Battery Park, after a matinee — I've been hooked on them ever since. Also, on two-show days, which I learned that everyone calls "two dow shays," or days with rehearsal before or after the show, we all hung out between. We had pot-luck lunches on the grass or made trips to the deli and sat at our cozy picnic tables, occasionally playing Bananagrams. Sometimes Rachel and I took long strolls along the waterfront together, other times a big group of us would head to the nearby mall to window shop. One time,

Raquel and I even found a glass carousel to ride on, a little walk away from the theatre. We all spent a lot of time together by choice because we had grown to love each other so much. Sure, some people clashed and bickered on occasion, as all families do, but the minute "Tradition" started every day we became an unwavering family. Every day, we came to the theatre with the joy, heart, and determination to tell our beautiful story. We all were so happy to be there, and we supported each other the entire way through. As the youngest of the bunch, I was constantly learning, and I sometimes felt like I was running twice as fast just to keep up with everyone. Every single thing was new to me, which was both exciting and terrifying. I had an entire family of a cast inspiring me, guiding me, and overflowing my spirit with passion every day. It was a group of the most special, good-hearted individuals, who, combined, existed as a beautiful family.

About a month into the run, our assistant choreographer, Merete, hosted a summer rooftop party at her apartment. I was in my apartment, about to leave to go to the party, when I decided I should make myself a snack first. I pulled out the avocado I had bought at the grocery store after trying one at the restaurant and loving it. I had never prepared an avocado before, though, so I called my roommate in from the other room to teach me how. She handed me a giant knife and told me how to cut it around the pit and then twist it open. Misjudging the consistency of the avocado, I instead cut right through the pit and into my left thumb. I hit an artery and got blood all over the kitchen. I texted Kat from the urgent care with my right hand to tell her I wouldn't be able to put pressure on my left hand for some time, while the doctor covered the length of my thumb with seven stitches. The next day everyone had to get to the theatre a few minutes early to re-work some of my set moves and hand holding. I was in a lot of pain, and it was really hard to do simple things. Luckily, I had the most supportive team behind me. Everyone took on extra set moves for me and were very gentle with my hands. Jodi and I giggled over holding pinkies in "Tradition," and Ben made a little bandage out of tape to put on my doll's thumb so that she matched me. Raquel braided my hair for me for several days, and Rachel tied my shmata and my apron. Rachel's husband, Seth, even bought me a special, soft knife for cutting avocados, which is the only knife I will ever use when cutting an avocado now. The highlight of the incident was Joel coming to the theatre, giving me a big hug, and asking, with fake crying noises, "Is this because I made you suck your thumb? Is it my fault?" Suffice to say, I never had to suck my thumb again — it was the end of an era.

* * *

Rachel Calter

Stage Manager

I am the Stage Manager, so my job is to run the deck and make sure everything is consistent and safe. Before the show, I walk around backstage with a big list and check to make sure that everyone has done their jobs and all of the props are set correctly. During the show I make sure that the vibe is good backstage, and that everything is as consistent as possible. I talk on a headset that has two channels: Channel A, and Channel B. Channel A connects everyone who is on a wireless headset, which is Team Wardrobe (Tim Peters, Sarah Dixie, Rose Labarre) and I, with our Production Stage Manager Kat West. This way we can hear Kat calling the show and if anything goes wrong, we can troubleshoot from backstage. For example, if something gets dropped or misplaced onstage that I wouldn't be able to see from the wings, Kat can notify me and then I can send someone on in the next scene to pick it up. Channel B is just the people on the wireless headset; most of that channel involves quick notices of people forgetting props or costume pieces, or needing an ice pack, and figuring out who can run and help them. It's a lot of boots on the ground problem solving. We're also mishpokhe, so when the show is running smoothly, we sometimes talk about other things, like cute bathing suits, on that channel. If something goes wrong backstage during the show, it is my job to problem solve.

In "The Dream" there is a kabuki curtain that drops for the actors to create shadows and dance behind. I had a plan for if the kabuki didn't drop, or fell early for some reason, but I never thought to have a plan for if the kabuki got stuck midway in the air and there was no way to get it down. During one show, the kabuki got stuck on a light, so it was halfway up and halfway down. I immediately went and grabbed the crew to ask what we could do. They wanted to be able to fly the kabuki all the way out, but unfortunately the cable was too short so that didn't work. We had to briefly hold the show, Mark Vogeley and I pulled on ropes to pull the electric away from the flats so it could be flown in. Then Mark pulled the kabuki free from the electric and we continued as normal.

One of the weirdest mishaps we have had was while we were running downtown at the National Yiddish Theatre Folksbiene. At the Folksbiene, we had to come in through the back door on Saturdays because the Museum of Jewish Heritage was closed. There was one day when I walked in through the back door and I noticed that there was this little line of sand that went all the way from security, across the tile, down the hallway, to the backstage area. There was a giant pile of sand right in the backstage area with one tiny footprint in it. We had no idea what it was or where it came from. We eventually got maintenance to come and sweep up the sand, but we didn't realize that maintenance didn't vacuum the hallway, which was entirely carpeted. During "To Life" we found out that the stage was slippery and realized that everybody who was walking in and out of the dressing room was stepping on the carpet and tracking sand onto the stage. We still had to do "The Dream," in which Jodi Snyder is up in the air on someone's shoulders, I think it was Grant Richards at that point, as the ghost of Frume Sore. It was pretty scary to have a stage with slippery sand on it before that number. We taped towels down right after the hallway and made everyone wipe their shoes before going onstage, so luckily by the time "The Dream" happened, it was all clear. The origin of the sand, and the tiny footprint, remains a mystery.

My favorite part of my job is spending time with people backstage, often making up little dances. I would never want to be the production stage manager, because I don't like feeling that detached from people during the run of the show. I love being backstage with everyone and getting to know people that way. Some of my favorite traditions during the show are the little dance I do with Samantha Hahn and Raquel Nobile before their "Matchmaker" entrance and shimmying with Jonathan Quigley and Nick Raynor before their scene shift at the end of that number. Another one of my favorite traditions is with Jackie Hoffman when she comes offstage during "The Rumor." She's the only one offstage with me during that part of the show, and we practice her choreographed hand moves for the last verse right before she goes onstage to do them. What's really fun is that we do it in a different way each day depending on how she is feeling or what is going on. Sometimes when it has been a long day, we do the hand moves like zombies or while doing the can-can to wake us up. There are a lot of people involved in the show and sometimes you don't get to see everyone before it starts, so it's nice to have special moments where you get to check in. And less people are late for entrances if they know they have a dance to do before them!

It's beautiful to come to work every day with people who are not only your coworkers but are also your friends. Sometimes that dynamic can be hard, but I feel so lucky to have gained many friendships here. One relationship I have formed through *Fiddler* that is very meaningful to me is with Lindsay Jones, who was the Assistant Stage Manager on our team downtown. We grew very close over those six months, and it's a friendship and a mentorship that is very special to me. When I first got my equity card, I was a junior in college, and it was the first thing I had ever done. I was very young, I was still in school, and there was a lot I didn't know. Lindsay is still in school, so it's really cool for me to learn about her program, and the things she is being taught differently, or the things she knows that I didn't when I was her age. As we started to work together and solidify as a team, we discovered a lot of similarities about our journeys as stage managers. We are both people who are invested in growing and learning and constantly improving our craft and ourselves, so as we learned more about each other, it became a very fulfilling relationship. We both teach and learn from one another, which is very special. We have all developed this silly, loving community, and every person that I connect with and dance with backstage is special to me.

* * *

Bobby Underwood

Role: Der Gradavoy | Ensemble

Playing the villain is cool in a lot of ways. It was hard at first because I'm essentially doing what people did to my own ancestors: I'm kicking Jewish families out of Russia. That was my family. It was the families of many people I know, and it was hard at first to get into that mindset. Joel gave me what sometimes seemed like contradictory notes, but looking back, the notes make a lot of sense because the Constable is complicated. In the book *Wonder of Wonders* that Alisa Solomon wrote about *Fiddler*, there is a passage where they talk about what kind of anti-Semite the Constable is. Does he hate Jews? Does he actually like Jews and hate doing his job but just has to do it? Is he a 'some of my best friends are Jews' type? I think they sort of settled on something in the middle there, and that seems to be where Joel and I have settled. To get into my character, I have a very specific person in mind when I talk to Tevye. I'm thinking of saying to him: *Look, I love you. You've done a lot for me. I hate to do this to you, but I've got to.*

I remember the first time Steven and I ran our scene. I was already confused because I didn't know we were going to run the scene in English first, and I was off book in Yiddish but not in English. I didn't want to spend time translating in my mind, so I got my script out. Acting with a script in hand is not easy and it was the first time I worked with Joel Grey. I wasn't yet in the place of saying, "Hey, Joel, what's going on, buddy?" This was *Joel Grey*. We were doing the scene and it wasn't going very well, and Joel turned to me and said, "You're the bad guy in this show. Did you know that?" I guess I got some sort of look on my face that made Steven come up to me at the end of rehearsal and ask if I was okay, which I was. Then the first time we ran the "Get Thee Out" scene, which is where I tell Tevye he has three days to get out of Anatevka, Joel privately said to me, "You're Hitler." A few days later we were working on the scene again, and Joel said to me, "You're not Hitler." This made me think, *Wait a minute, what? Which do you want?* Now, looking back I see what he was doing. Joel knew how to get the Constable's inner conflict out of me.

The Tree of Life synagogue shooting happened while we were running downtown in the Museum of

Jewish Heritage. It probably hurt me more than any other shooting since Sandy Hook. I think the worst thing about America these days — and there's a lot of competition — is how commonplace shootings are. It is truly awful. Yesterday there was a school shooting in Colorado that barely made the news. Twenty years ago, the shooting at Columbine was all over the news for months. For the longest time, there were just three stories in the news: baseball home run chase, Bill Clinton's impeachment, and the Columbine shooting. That was all anybody talked about. Today we get more news stories than that in just one hour. We get numb. It's terrible, but we get numb to these shootings, and we are just glad it isn't happening to us and the people we love. Then there's a shooting in a synagogue that looks an awful lot like your synagogue, and it un- numbs you. That shooting really affected me. It affected all of us, especially doing this show. I think it's impossible for a tragedy like that not to bring us closer together.

* * *

Bruce Sabbath

Role: Leyzer-Volf | Tevye Understudy

The Folksbiene had never really been involved with the Broadway Cares Equity Fights Aids organization in the past. I had been involved before with other shows in the city, so I thought, *Why not get Fiddler involved?* We started with the Broadway Run, which had only been around for a few years. I'm a runner so it was something that I had been excited to be a part of in the past. There had never been a show with a team for the Broadway Run before. The people who ran it said, "Are you serious? You can get actual actors who are principal characters in your show to run this race and raise money?" They were so thrilled. We had thirteen people from both the cast and crew participating in the Broadway Run and raising money for Broadway Cares. We were the first actual show that had a team, and the second top fundraising team in the run.

That race led right into the fundraising for the Red Bucket Follies in the fall. We started right away with giving speeches after the shows, collecting with the red buckets in the lobby, and everyone raising money, with the help of our generous audiences. We only had three weeks to do it because we had started late and we were closed for a week in late October. During that week, the terrible shooting at the Tree of Life Synagogue in Pittsburgh occurred. When we came back to the theatre, people from the cast and the creative team were already talking about what we could do to help. We knew we had to do something. We contacted an organization in Pittsburgh that we could send money to, and then we worked with Broadway Cares in order to send funds to them. For the next week we raised money exclusively for the community in Pittsburgh, and we were able to send fifteen thousand dollars to them. In all, we raised forty-three thousand dollars which was more than any other Off-Broadway show.

We closed downtown and re-opened uptown and soon it was time to start collecting money again for the Broadway Cares Easter Bonnet Competition. Everybody was right back on board, collecting and doing speeches. We started the very first day allowed and collected until the very last day. The last day of fundraising we thought it would be neat to get Joel Grey to come in and auction him off. Ben Liebert was our auctioneer, and we auctioned an experience for an audience member to come up onstage and have Joel Grey serenade them. We started with a couple hundred dollars, and it seemed like it was going slow at first but then it just kept going. In the end there were two people who were going back and forth, getting closer and closer to a thousand dollars. Ben suggested, "Would both of you be willing to be winners for a thousand dollars? Each of you can get a song, you each get to come onstage, and then you both can take pictures with everyone backstage." They said yes. Joel sang his "When I was Eight Days Old" song to the first person, and "Willkommen" to the second person. The cast joyfully backed him up for "Willkommen" with "oompas". Then Joel said, "Anyone else want a song?"

Someone raised their hand, matched the donation of a thousand dollars, and was serenaded with "Give My Regards to Broadway."

In addition to the fundraising, we prepped a lot for the skit for the Easter Bonnet Competition. We rehearsed at the theatre between shows. Ben and Adam had created this skit called "Better in Yiddish," about what other famous musicals would be like if we did them in Yiddish. It was a bunch of short snippets of musicals, one after the other. It ended with Joel singing "Give My Regards to Broadway" in Yiddish. It was such an exciting couple of days, and very frenetic. The first day we had to go in and tech the number really quickly. We only had a few minutes on stage with the lights and the orchestrations, and we ran the number through twice. Then we got to actually perform it for an audience of sixteen hundred people. The audience was screaming. I've never heard or been a recipient of that kind of applause. It was so loud that we knew we did something right. They announced that we won best presentation, and we ran out onstage and got presented a plaque by some pretty mind-blowing people including Jeff Daniels, Bryan Cranston, Kelli O'Hara, and Glenda Jackson. Then they announced the fundraising portion. *Avenue Q* had raised the most money at every Broadway Cares event they participated in since they moved to their Off-Broadway home, so when they announced that *Avenue Q* was the runner-up, we knew we were going to win. It was a lot of work, but we ended up raising seventy-seven thousand dollars for Broadway Cares, more than any other Off-Broadway show. Bryan Cranston danced over with the second plaque, and he gave it to Ben who handed it to me. Then Lin-Manuel Miranda himself leaped onto the stage to accept his plaque for the most money raised in total for the Hamilton tour and came over to give Joel a big hug. The thing about this Fiddler is the strong sense of mishpokhe that we have. I think something about the origin of the show, doing it in Yiddish, and Joel Grey's warmth has brought the group together. That's what makes it so easy to come together for things like this.

The "littles" backstage during a show at Stage 42.
From left to right: Raquel Nobile, Samantha Hahn.

At the Folksbiene, with prints of the original
Ann Hould-Ward costume sketches gifted to the oldest daughters.
From left to right: Rachel Zatcoff, Stephanie Mason, Rosie Jo Nedd , Joel Grey.

The first day of rehearsal at the National Yiddish Theatre Folksbiene.
Top row: Rosie Jo Neddy, Stephanie Lynne Mason, Mary Illes, Joel
Grey, Steven Skybell, Jackie Hoffman, Rachel Zatcoff.
Bottom row: Samantha Hahn, Raquel Nobile.

Frume Sore rehearsing "The Dream" at Ripley Grier Studios.
From top to bottom: Jodi Snyder, Evan Mayer.

Reading about Yiddish backstage during a show.
From left to right: Mikhl Yashinsky, Evan Mayer.

The sisters bonding at Yiddish Under the Stars in Central Park.
Top row: Samantha Hahn, Raquel Nobile, Rosie Jo Neddy.
Bottom row: Stephanie Lynne Mason, Rachel Zatcoff

The boys with Joel at the first sitzprobe
Top row: Evan Mayer, Nick Raynor.
Bottom row: Joshua Dunn, Joel Grey, Cameron Johnson, James Števko.

The oldest daughter and youngest daughter at Sardi's for the opening night party.
From left to right: Rachel Zatcoff, Samantha Hahn.

The bottle dancers rehearsing at Ripley Grier Studios.
From left to right: Joshua Dunn, Nick Raynor, James Števko, Evan Mayer.

The sisters in costume for the first time before tech rehearsal
From left to right: Rachel Zatcoff, Stephanie ynne Mason,
Rosie Jo Neddy, Raquel Nobile, Samantha Hahn.

The women of Tevye's family in the dressing room at the Folksbiene. From left to right: Rachel Zatcoff, Stephanie ynne Mason, Rosie Jo Neddy, Raquel Nobile, Samantha Hahn, Jennifer Babiak.

Joel goofing around on stage during a rehearsal break
From left to right: Adam Shapiro, Joel Grey.

A between show picnic in Battery Park for Evan's last day.
From left to right: Tim Peters, Kayleen Seidl, Jodi Snyder, Raquel Nobile,
Samantha Hahn, Rachel Zatcoff, Stephanie ynne Mason.

The Fiddler BCEFA running team outside the Folksbiene.

The sisters in braids to celebrate my last show.
From left to right: Rosie Jo Neddy, Stephanie Lynne Mason, Rachel Zatcoff,
Samantha Hahn, Raquel Nobile.

Rehearsal on the stage at the Folksbiene.
From left to right: Kirk Geritano, Bobby Underwood,
Drew Seigla, Michael Einav, John Giesige.

Snuggling in the elevator at Slic Studios after the photoshoot with Mathew Murphy.
Top row: Samantha Hahn, Steven Skybell, Joel Grey.
Bottom row: Rachel Zatcoff, Raquel Nobile, Rosie Jo Nedd , Stephanie Lynne Mason.

The initial audition table.
From left to right: Christopher Massimine, Jamibeth Margolis, Merete Muenter,
Staś Kmieć, Joel Grey, Zalmen Mlotek, Motl Didner.

In the elevator with Joel after a long day of rehearsal at Ripley Grier Studios.
From left to right: Lauren Thomas, Samantha Hahn, Joel Grey,
Rachel Zatcoff, Bruce Sabbath, Adam B. Shapiro.

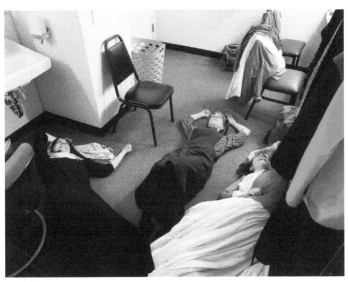

The star ladies collapsing on the floor of their dressing room at intermission.
From left to right: Jennifer Babiak, Jackie Hoffman, Rachel Zatcoff

Motl and Tsaytl in their wedding costumes on stage for tech rehearsal at Stage 42.
From left to right: Ben Liebert, Rachel Zatcoff.

Tevye and Tsaytl backstage after the hundredth show at Stage 42.
From left to right: Steven Skybell, Rachel Zatcoff.

Joel tickling me at the Minskoff theatre before the BCE A Easter Bonnet Competition.
From left to right: Joel Grey, Samantha Hahn.

Backstage besties sitting on the milk jug during "Do You Love Me".
From left to right: Rachel Zatcoff, Samantha Hahn.

Part Nine
Zay Gezunt

Sammy

Role: Beylke

Fiddler on the Roof in Yiddish was supposed to be a summer show. I thought it would be perfect timing for me, because my junior year of college, studying musical theatre at Manhattan School of Music, would begin in the fall. The show ended up doing so well that we added a week of performances on to our original closing date. For me, this meant missing orientation week and placement auditions at school, which I managed to make work with support from the new head of our theatre program. Then, something really unexpected happened. Towards the end of the original run downtown at the National Yiddish Theatre Folksbiene, the producers and creative team called the full company to the house for an important meeting after a show. We sat in the theatre seats whispering to each other, sharing meaningful glances, and spreading rumors of what was to come. A common guess was that we were going to extend the show for an additional week due to popular demand. We had no idea how much of a hit our Yiddish *Fiddler* was actually becoming. They announced that the show was going to run for another month, and hopefully even continue after that. It was thrilling beyond belief; we all cheered and cried. We couldn't believe that our little shtetl was taking the world by storm. I yelped with joy, but after a moment of excitement, I was overcome with conflict. I suddenly had a difficult decision to make. I immediately sent an email to the new head of my program at school, asking if there was any way for me to continue with *Fiddler* during the start of the school year. She quickly emailed me back to say that the most I could do was one extra week of *Fiddler*. If I wanted to continue with the show after that, I would have to take a year-long leave of absence from college.

I was in no way ready or wanting to leave school, but leaving the show when it was still running was a devastating thought. I still felt like I had so much to learn, both at school and at *Fiddler*, and I was completely at war with myself. Aside from that, I was scared. If I took a leave of absence, it was possible that *Fiddler* would close after a month and then I would have nothing to do for an entire year. I would be held back a grade, unable to graduate with my class, and when the show ended, I would be out on my butt with no job, no classes, and no clue what to do. I was also scared that if I went back to school, *Fiddler* would transfer to Broadway without me, it would be the biggest regret of my life, and I would never get to be in a show again. The wheels in my head were turning at lightning speed. I had only a couple of days to decide what I was going to do, so I used that time to talk to all the people whose advice I thought might help me. I talked to my family, friends from home, friends from school, teachers, and *Fiddler* castmates. There was no general consensus: some people told me I had to go to school, other people told me I had to stay with the show. Most people, along with these opinions, told me that either way I would be fine, and that the decision wouldn't make or break my career or my life. I had to go with my gut and make the choice for myself. I would like to say that I let my heart fully guide the decision, but I can't honestly claim that fear didn't play a factor. The truth is my gut felt a lot calmer choosing the path I had already planned. I expected to do *Fiddler* over the summer and then return to college with an amazing experience and Off-Broadway credit under my belt, so that was the option that felt solid to me. Though it broke my heart, I decided to leave *Fiddler* early.

I wasn't the only one in the cast who had to make this decision. Mikhl Yashinsky was a teacher, so he also had to return to school, Daniel Kahn was getting married, and Kayleen Seidl, Joshua Dunn, and Evan Mayer all had other shows lined up perfectly with the end of the original run. Evan left a few days after the original closing date, followed by Dan a couple days later, and then Kayleen, Josh, and Mikhl all left after the original one-week extension. I stayed a week longer, which was the longest I was allowed by school, missing orientation week and the first week of classes. The day that Evan left the show was very emotional. Aside from Mary Illes, who we knew wasn't staying with us for the full original run, Evan was the first to leave. We had two shows that day, and between shows the whole cast had a lunchtime picnic in the field of grass outside the theatre. We laid on a picnic blanket in the grass, having lunch, listening to music, munching on Oreos, and saying goodbye to a member of our *Fiddler* family. Before "places" was called for the evening show, we gathered in the hallway to sing "Happy Trails" to Evan. Everyone was crying extra hard in the "Exodus" scene; we were saying goodbye in real life, as well as in the show, to someone who felt like a family member. During the curtain call we gave Evan an extra push forward and cheered for him as he took his final *Fiddler* bow with us at the National Yiddish Theatre Folksbiene. Joel was there to give him a happy farewell, and we took him out to celebrate after. It was the first of the goodbyes.

The day after Evan left the show, orientation week began at school. My friends were suddenly all back from their summer breaks, and I was getting emails every second about curriculum, teachers, required reading, schedules, and all things school- related. We had gotten a new head of our theatre program over the summer, and along with her came many new teachers and other changes. Meanwhile, the shtetl was changing too. With Evan gone, Dan leaving within days, only a week left before Kayleen, Josh, and Mikhl would leave, and only two weeks before I was leaving, new cast members were needed. Along with replacements for those of us who were departing, they were hiring offstage swings to better cover for cast absences in the extended run. We got to meet all of the new cast members at a big understudy "put in" rehearsal. We decided to make the rehearsal "pajama-themed" for fun, so we all wore our best sleepwear to run through the show, with different understudies coming up to do different roles. We were running "Tradition" onstage when the new cast members started trickling in from the back of the theatre. They took their seats, notebooks and binders in hand, and began watching us, taking notes and studying the show. After "Tradition," we paused the rehearsal and met all of our new cast members. They were extremely friendly and excited to be there, and we were just as excited to meet them. Joel brought them onstage with us and had us all get in a big circle, and then made a short and sweet speech about the realism of the show, and the closeness of the cast. It was the perfect way to welcome everyone in and introduce them to our special little family.

When Daniel Kahn left the show, a few performances after Grant Richards took over for Evan, the wonderful Drew Seigla joined the company to fill the role of Perchik. Tevye, Golde, and the daughters came in to have a short rehearsal with him prior to his full company rehearsal of being put into the show. This involved running Act One, Scene Six with him, as well as "Sabbath Prayer," and the scene prior to that. It also involved Rosie and Raquel dancing and belting out "I will survive" on the stage before he got there, which is only important because I laughed so hard I thought I would pee myself, and I continually look back at the video I took of them for a good laugh. Drew's put-in rehearsal with the full company was the following week, during the first day of orientation at school. I went to the first half of orientation during the day and missed rehearsal, and then went to the theatre to do the show and missed the rest of the school day.

Being at school again felt really strange, and the orientation was not as fun as I had hoped. I was overwhelmed with questions and odd statements related to being in *Fiddler*. A lot of students casually, and maybe jokingly, mentioned being "jealous" of me, which I had no idea how to respond to. Others made odd statements about how I was "getting out of" the first week of school, which made me feel uncomfortable too. Some of my teachers put me on the spot with highly expectant questions about my experience, of which I had not prepared answers. I was getting too much unwanted attention, in very unsettling ways. On top of all of this, I was meeting dozens of new students and teachers, being hugged and gushed at by people who had scarcely acknowledged me in the past, and I was already missing my cast. Rushing back to the theatre felt like the biggest relief ever. The cast was on a food break when I got back, and I was texting Rachel on the way to let her know my estimated time of arrival. When I got to the theatre, we ran to each other into a huge hug. We immediately took a little stroll by the water to catch up on our days apart: she told me that it was so weird not having me at rehearsal, and I told her how strange my orientation felt. She had a lot of wise words and advice for me, as she always does, and by the time we started the show I felt a lot better. At the end of the week, I cried as we sang "Happy Trails" to Kayleen, Josh, and Mikhl, losing three of the biggest hearts in the cast, and knowing that in a week I would be taking my last bow.

It was raining on my last day at *Fiddler,* which felt like the sky crying for me. I got to the theatre extra early to leave little gifts and cards on everyone's stations, and posted a poem I wrote for the cast on the callboard:

Dear Wonderful Cast of Fiddler,

Thank you to my cast, you fill me with glee, you've all been the very best mishpokhe to me: To Bruce and the bestest pool party in town,

To Mikhl for making it impossible to frown. To Joanne for being the dressing room mom, To Michael for being the absolute bomb,

To Abby for being the sweetest and so great, To Jess for being amazing, first rate,

To Lisa for smiling through every endeavor, To Cam for holding that note for forever,

To Adam for being the flyest rabbi yet, To Kirk for

the rumor you'll never forget, To Grant for always being ready to go, To Quigs for the way you just glow,

To Bobby for all the massages and fun, To Josh for shining brighter than the sun, To Drew for all the fun lessons every day, To John for having the friendliest way,

To Moshe for being so enthralling with a flair,

To Maya, whom I cannot wait to see up there, To Evan for all of the best videos,

To Dan for keeping us all on our toes,

To James for dancing his pants off each night, To Nick for being a ball of love and light,

To Kayleen for the emergency chocolates and love, To Jackie for laughter that rises above,

To Mary for being so lovely and grand,

To Ben for the word games and squeezing my hand, To Steph for all of the baking and care,

To Rosie for being a breath of fresh air, To Steven for inspiring me to no end,

To Lauren for being the realest, great friend, To Jodi for being my bud from the start,

To Jen for having the world's biggest heart,

To Raquel, you're my rock, my partner in crime,

To Rachel, I life you, there's not enough time,

Each and every one of you will sincerely be missed, And, if you go to Broadway without me, I'll be pissed, Come visit me at school and I'll be back here a ton, Thank you so much for this amazing run!

Love, Sammy

Rachel met me early at the cafe above the theatre to have breakfast, and we exchanged meaningful gifts, cards, and a lot of hugs. Part of her gift to me was a box of Louise Hay's power thought cards, and her favorite book. She had me read the book right at the breakfast table, and it immediately became one of my favorite books too. My gift to her was a homemade box of Mary Oliver cards — quotes from her favorite poet that she had been sharing with me. When we went down to the dressing room, I was showered with even more gifts. Raquel got me the best Pure Barre socks with little stars on them, because we always talked about Pure Barre together. I made her a special box and a picture frame of us, and we exchanged the sweetest cards. I gave Jodi a little sign that said, "I love you more than Ice Cream," and she got me chocolate milk and wheat thins, which I always snacked on at the theatre. Lauren got me a unicorn pencil case with a special note on the back of it, and Jen got me a pretty little unicorn keychain, because I have a thing for unicorns. Stephanie made me Rice Krispie treats, and Rosie brought me an ice cream cake — both my favorite treats. My mom and dad even sent me gifts and a card to the theatre for my last day.

Jodi had designed and ordered us all special *Fiddler* shirts with our characters' names on the back, and we had decided to wear them that day to take a group picture. We went on the stage to take the picture, and then the cast surprised me by pulling out a chair and lifting me up in it for a second picture. It was like Tsaytl in the wedding scene — a moment of pure joy. Then we gathered in the hallway and they sang "Happy Trails" to me. When they asked me to say a few words, I said, "I love you guys so much. Do the best show for me today." Before the show, instead of pulling power thought cards, Rachel surprised me by pulling out the box of Mary Oliver cards I made her. We went around the room reading the beautiful poetry of Mary Oliver, which moved a lot of us to tears. The show itself went by far too quickly. Raquel had the task of pushing me out to take an extra bow at the end, which I did through streaming tears. When it was over, we all went out to eat and celebrate my last show. While we were celebrating and saying goodbye, Raquel helped everyone put their hair in two braids, in honor of how I wore it in the show. I made my "show sisters" promise to steal Baby Beylke, my doll, for me whenever the show closed. We laughed and lamented, and then we had to leave. I cried the whole subway ride home, as only a real New Yorker does. On the way back to my apartment, I got an email from Joel Grey. It said: "Your sweet and honest presence in our play was always so special! So talented! Will miss you, for sure! Xxxxx"

When I got home, I packed up my bag for school with my binder, notebooks, my *Fiddler* pencil case that said "Vayt fun mayn liber heym," which means "Far from the home I love," the sparkly pen from Rosalind Harris, my box of Louise Hay's power thought cards, and the book Rachel gave me. I was already feeling "vayt fun mayn liber heym," so I re-read the beautiful notes from my castmates and lifelong friends. One line from Rachel's note to me said: "You carry each show, each role, each cast with you — forever. It's one of the most generous and wonderful parts of this business." I went back to school the next morning with a full heart, and the support of a shtetl behind me.

* * *

Abby Goldfarb

Role: Female Swing

The first time I met Joel was at the first big rehearsal after the extension downtown that the incoming cast members were attending. I was watching the rehearsal of the original cast members with the new cast members and taking notes. Joel had everyone come on stage and get in a big circle. He looked around and said, "For the new members that are joining us… this show is not shtick. It's life." Then he explained what the show was with a series of gestures essentially. I was in awe. He made it such an intimate environment from the rehearsal room to the stage. I immediately felt like I got the feeling we were striving for.

There are a lot of pros and cons to being a swing. At first it was really challenging, but it's an amazing challenge to have to know where everyone is at all times. All of the parts I cover stand next to each other during the group numbers, which is crazy. I have to have my eye on everything and know all the choreography for the different roles. It's a really good brain exercise. I'll find out at the last minute that I'm going on, or maybe the day before, and it's very exciting. I don't get bored ever, and it's never stale because I'm always on my toes. At the same time, when I'm not in the show, there is a lot of downtime. It's hard to stay energetic with all the sitting. At half hour, when everyone is getting into costume, I eat. That's my dinner or lunchtime depending on if it's a matinee or evening show. If I know I'm going on for a role soon, I watch the show from backstage. We have a TV that has a live stream of the show, which is a great way to track what I'm doing. Or most of the time I'm singing backstage and doing puzzles. I have my own table in the dressing room, and it has been filled with many a puzzle; I've done six so far.

After memorizing everything, keeping things fresh is almost a day-to-day thing. If I'm in for someone that day, it does require me to sometimes think, *Okay, who am I next to in Tradition? Who do I pass in this number?* And it's great because I do have the opportunity to just check in and then visually remember everything. It's kind of scary because pretty much all my tracks are in my head — I don't really have a script to show anyone my tracks. Maybe that's why my brain has liked being a swing, because I can kind of see it all, which is cool.

Frume Sore is my favorite role to practice, and I think that would be my favorite role to go on for. I think that would be everyone's favorite too. Who doesn't want to go up on someone's shoulders and be evil and scream? Honestly, it's just really fun to be onstage and be a part of the shtetl for three hours since I don't get to do it every day. The first time I went on was a split track role, half of the Bobe Tsaytl track and half of the Sheyndl track. I just remember hearing the: "DUN DUN DUN Traditsye!" Then I was just thinking, *Oh my god, I'm onstage.* I don't remember half of it. I was just very happy I got through it and found my place.

A lot has happened in my life this past year, including the fact that I got married. I had only been with the show for a few months at the time, but the whole cast surprised me with a wedding party. I wasn't even having a big ceremony or any kind of big party, so it meant a lot to me. Adam Shapiro baked a cake for me, and it felt so special to have that big life moment with the support of the entire cast. I guess it just shows how special this group of people is and how close we are. It's probably overdone to say that Steven Skybell is an incredible Tevye... but he is an incredible Tevye. Watching him every day is truly like taking an acting class. It's a breath of fresh air to see him do such a well-known part in a way that I've never seen before. He really breaks down all of the possible barriers and stereotypes, and he lives the role with such ease and vulnerability. My favorite memory is that for opening night Joel made each of us a *Fiddler* hat with his initials and our initials on the back of it. There was something so simple and meaningful about that gift; it is something that I will keep forever.

* * *

Moshe Lobel

Role: Male Swing | Nokhum | Mordkhe

I auditioned four times for this production. I went to the first open call and couldn't get in, but I bumped into the associate director and Yiddish coach Motl Didner when I was there, and he said he could get me an appointment later on. I got an appointment for a chorus call, and then got a call-back for a dance call. I didn't get it from that, but I was working on another project so it was okay at the time. In August, I got an email from the casting director Jamibeth Margolis looking for a Perchik for a one-week extension of the show. As a native Yiddish speaker, I thought I had a very good chance since it was a big track to learn at the last minute. I actually met Drew Seigla, who ended up getting the role of Perchik, on the elevator ride up to the audition. The audition was very cool because I got to read with Stephanie Lynne Mason, who plays Hodl. Stephanie is such a giving actress, so I was able to work off of her rather than working with the very important people sitting behind the table. I didn't get the role of Perchik, of course, but I got called in a week later for an ensemble role because they were extending again. I had some conflicts that I told Jamibeth about, and I thought I wasn't going to go. I was thinking, *you've seen me do this before, what else could I even show you?* I didn't want to schlep into the city, but everyone I know, including my mom, told me I had to go to get a chance to work with Joel Grey. I went in and did the material they asked me to prepare, and then I did a dance call that didn't go very well for me because I don't have any musical theatre training. I left thinking I didn't get it, but since I was already there, I decided to stay to watch the show. As soon as the opening number "Tradition" started I thought, *I should've tried harder at my audition.* It really blew me away. There is a reason that it is a hit. When I got the offer the next day, I immediately took it.

It's always challenging to come into a company that has been working and developing a show together. You're coming in to a fully finished product. When I was a kid, I had to switch schools a lot so that really prepared me for this. I had to learn how to adapt and join a class that has been growing together. It was pretty fun here because I ran into Drew the first day, and we were both glad that we had each gotten into the production. I also met some of the other new cast members for the extension at the auditions and callbacks, so it was nice to have an incoming class to jump in with. The cast ended up being really welcoming, and I immediately felt like they were ready to try to get to know me. When I was playing Mordkhe, one of my favorite things was being the host of two scenes: the bar scene in "To Life" and the wedding scene at the end of the first act. As Mordkhe, I enjoyed this "hosting" and being responsible for everyone having a good time. Now, as an understudy I enjoy discovering how each of my characters interacts with the others throughout the show, all the different relationships. It was really fun to get to connect with different people from the cast really personally throughout the show.

* * *

Kat West

Production Stage Manager

The biggest thing about being the production stage manager of *Fiddler* is that it never stops. Even when things are running well, there is constant motion, someone to touch base with, an additional consideration to add, rehearsals, backstage life, special events, special guests, etc. Basically, there's something to be managed at every point in time.

On a typical show day, I communicate with people, problem solve, do paperwork, and call the show. In the morning, if there is anyone who needs to call out of the show for illness, they communicate it to me first. I then tell our deck stage manager, Rachel Calter, and the wardrobe team, and we confirm who is going to be on in that role and if it requires multiple people to be on. Once that is set, the covers are informed. Then an email goes out to the full company, crew, front of house staff, and producers to let them know the casting for the day. Throughout the day there is normally either Yiddish coaching or rehearsal and always a lot of paperwork. The paperwork includes documentations to update, actor hours to track, cut-combo reports, incident reports, and schedules, just to name a few. The crew is called to the theatre an hour and a half before the show, and I check in with the front of house staff and everyone at the theatre when we get there. I make sure that the house board by the box office has all the roles listed correctly for that show and that we have enough stuffers for the playbills.

Before "half hour" we run anything that needs to be done for safety, such as the pogrom call or the wedding chairlifts. We do a final blackout check and turn the house over to our house manager who lets in the patrons. Then the time calls begin: half hour to curtain, fifteen minutes, five minutes, and finally places. Between those calls I check in with every dressing room to see how everyone is, and if there are changes to the run of show for that performance, I review the changes with the company based off of change lists that Rachel Calter has prepared and I've double checked. During half hour I also check in with company management about any preapproved actor absences or any other cast, crew, or orchestral needs. Once "places" is called, I settle into my calling station, which is off Stage Right, and wait for the company to get set and for the house manager to turn the house over to us. I check in with our sound mixer, light board and supertitle operators, and conductor. Then, off we go. I am responsible for calling all the light and sound cues during the show as well as cueing some of the deck action via cue lights.

The biggest challenge of this show for me was not the Yiddish, believe it or not, but navigating my role as a production stage manager while being a new mom. My son, Rafael, was a little over three months old when we started *Fiddler* downtown, and at our one-year anniversary he is now over sixteen months old. *Fiddler* is all encompassing, as is a new baby, so trying to be my best for both has been tough. I have been very fortunate to have such a supportive and understanding cast, crew, and creative team who kept their faith in me to lead the production through tech, the run, and extension after extension while navigating the role of a first-time parent. My husband, Jaime, also deserves so much credit for being the ultimate "shtetl spouse," as the back of his Fiddler t-shirt says.

The most supportive person of all throughout this is our director, Joel Grey. It was a tad intimidating to go to work for him and to support his vision — not because he is intimidating, but because of the legacy he carries and the many amazing people he has worked with. The director/production stage manager relationship is very important, and my working relationship with Joel is one of the best I have ever had. The mutual respect and trust that we give and take from each other is a dream. Our relationship got solidified during tech week. I was still breastfeeding my son, so I spent most of the downtown run having to pump milk several times a day — in rehearsal, out of rehearsal, and all throughout tech. One day we were tech-ing "The Dream," which is the most technically complicated number in the show. As we worked through it, I was pumping, calling, running cue lights, and timing with a stopwatch. I kept running out of hands. It was also stressful for our actors who play Frume Sore because they have to be stacked on each other and it's very tiring. Many concerns and questions were flying at me from all sides, and I was pumping away at the same time and announcing, "OK, four issues just came up in the last ten seconds; we'll address this first, this second..." and so on. We got through all of it and took a break. On the break right after I cleaned up and put my milk away, Joel came up to me with a question. I don't remember the question, only that it wasn't overly important in that moment, and I just needed a little break. I got very flip, which is unlike me, and said, "I don't know, Joel. I just pump milk here!" Our costume designer, Ann Hould-Ward, and her associate, Amy Price, were sitting at the tech table behind me and they burst out laughing. Joel kind of froze for a second, and then I froze for being sassy to him. But he looked and me and got a little smirk on his face and said, "That was good! Very well done," and he walked away with his question unanswered. I knew from that point I could just be my honest self with him, no matter what, and we'd be OK. He trusted me, and we've had that kind of relationship ever since.

One of my favorite memories of rehearsal downtown was our "Pajama put-in." We were welcoming five new people during that rehearsal and beginning to change from our summer cast to our fall cast, and I decided to theme the put-in to make it more fun. The cast got really into it, as they do with everything. Colorful PJs abounded, and it made the rehearsal go quickly. Even though the put-ins were challenging, like any challenge with this company, we find a way to get the work done and have fun with each other.

The only word I can think of to describe this *Fiddler* experience is *special.* It doesn't do nearly enough but it's the best I can come up with. Putting up this show in the time we had in a language that was foreign to most of us was difficult. It bonded us in a way that no show I have ever worked on has. Everyone works just as hard and are just as focused today as they were when we started. We all put our whole hearts in because that is what Joel did, and what NYTF, our designers, creative team, crew, and Yiddish coaches do. We all knew that the story was important and resonant, and that telling it this way was unique. We all have so much love for our craft, each other, and the show, and that love transfers to our audience. This company is built on love. Our Tevye, Steven Skybell, sets such a wonderful tone for the company and leads by quiet example; he exemplifies the commitment that we all share to this story. The majority of us have stayed on since the beginning and kept with this show, and it has never gotten stale or tired. Sometimes we get frustrated or picky with each other, but we are a family and that's what families do. That doesn't happen all the time, so I'm happy for the people who are having this as their first big professional experience, but at the same time I'm concerned for them because not all shows are like this. This is one of the best, hardest, and most encompassing shows I've done in my life, and probably will ever do. No matter what changes we go through, the heart of this production stays the same. I've never been involved with a company and a show with as much heart as this. As tired as I can be some days, I still pinch myself that all of this heart is still beating strong and touching audiences in ways none of us expected. I'm very thankful and proud.

* * *

Jonathan Quigley

Role: Ensemble | Fiddler Understudy

This was the third time I joined a production in the middle of its run. Each cast has its different vibes. On my first day of work here, there was a "Pajama put-in" for the cast. I met everyone, including stage management, in their pajamas. It was a weird first impression, but it was really cool to get to know everyone in an informal way.

Moving uptown with the show and getting to watch Joel rehearse with Steven Skybell and Jennifer Babiak was one of the best things. I won't forget that. I remember one time there was a mini rehearsal for "Do You Love Me" before we started the day, and since I always get here early, I got to watch the whole thing. It was just Steven and Jen onstage, with Joel in the front row directing them. I was sitting on the other side of the front row, and I got to watch all the little moments and nuances in that scene. The hardest part, aside from the Yiddish, was the bottle dance. I did not actually get to put a bottle on my head until two days before I went on, which was very nerve-wracking. My favorite part of the show is the post-dance wedding scene. Most of the cast is on the stage, and it's so cool that we all get to be onstage in a scene together. That rarely happens.

I was so nervous the first few weeks of previews for the uptown transfer. I was a replacement from the

164

downtown production, so I really felt like I had just hopped on this moving train. I was worried that they were going to suddenly look at me in rehearsal and decide that I wasn't working well in the show. During the rehearsal process and tech week, I had never really heard anything from Joel or anyone specifically about how I was doing, so it was kind of eating at me. One day Joel was backstage, so during a run- through I went up to him and asked, "How am I doing? I have no idea. Is it working? Is it not working?" He just looked at me and said, "You're good. If you weren't, you would know." Opening night uptown was one of the most memorable experiences. Having a party at Sardi's was so crazy and clichéd and wonderful. I had never been there before, and I didn't realize how many photos there actually were. My mom and sister were there, and I was just so happy.

* * *

John Giesige

Role: Male Swing | Dance Captain

My audition was super weird because I was a replacement. We had a chorus call at Pearl Studios and did knee crawls for forty-five minutes straight. We were dying. Then the next day we did our final callback at the theatre. The team was sitting in the house watching us, and we had to go up on the National Yiddish Theatre Folksbiene stage and sing in Yiddish for them. Yiddish is actually easy for me because I've always had an ear for language. I can mock the accent that goes with it and then I can start faking my way through it until I get it. The hardest part of the show is "To Life." I don't think people realize that — I think everyone assumes the hardest part is the bottle dance. At this point, the bottle dance is easy. It's the least of my worries. "To Life" is so hard because we are doing many Russian feats of strength that people aren't meant to do one after the other. It's crazy and hard and literally talking about it is stressing me out. Then the Constable comes on the stage, and we have to stand there and can't breathe or move as if we haven't just finished a full cardio dance number.

Being the dance captain is both harder and easier than I thought. I've never had to learn any of the women's choreography in a show before. I love the little dance that the ladies do off to the side in the wedding scene, and I never would have fully noticed that if I didn't have to learn it. It's really fun to see something that is off or unfinished and finish it and make it look right. Even adjusting someone's spacing by one foot can change the whole picture. It's very cool. Staś Kmieć is an old-school choreographer. He tells you how to do the dance, and you do it. If it's not right you might get yelled at, because that's how old-school choreographers work. It's interesting as the dance captain to be the mouth of the cast. Sometimes I have to say: "We actually can't run this number again because we have to be able to do it in the show tonight." I have to go back and forth between being the support of the cast and the choreographer. Sometimes that involves having to stand up to someone above me that I respect. I've never had to do that before and it's such a challenging role.

There is so much camaraderie between all of us in the little moments on stage that no one notices. There are moments of eye contact and weird things we add into the scene changes to entertain ourselves. We always spot each other from across the wings when we are waiting to go on stage, and there will just be teams of people having dance parties. I feel like all of that just makes the onstage chemistry much more, full, and it wouldn't exist if we didn't get along as a cast like we do. That's something that I've noticed since my first day of rehearsal. Everyone was so nice and excited to meet me and just happy to be there. I knew it was going to be a good experience from that first day.

The first time I met Jackie Hoffman she walked into the boys' dressing room, and I said, "Hi, Jackie! I'm John!"

She just looked at me and said, "Hope you're not psychotic," and turned on her heel and walked out of the room. It was amazing. I was scared of her for so long. I didn't really know how to talk to her, or Joel. I still don't know how to talk to Joel, really. Jackie is so funny. She wasn't in "The Dream" downtown, but when we transferred uptown, she wanted to be put into it. That meant that I got an hour alone in a studio with her, teaching her the choreography and spacing. It took a full hour because she kept stopping to tell me stories. It was wild because my first survival job in New York City was handing out flyers in Times Square for *On the Town* on Broadway, which she was in. I was dressed as a sailor. I actually showed her a picture of me from that time and said, "Look, Jackie, I kept you guys open." It was a full-circle moment.

Part Ten
Heym

Sammy

Role: Beylke

The first thing I did when I went back to school was to get a haircut and paint my nails. In order to maintain the continuity of *Fiddler*, we weren't allowed to paint our nails or cut our hair because "there are no salons in Anatevka." I was back to being a college student: learning new things, sitting in classes all day long, dancing my pants off, doing homework, and writing essays. There were some classes that made me think there was nowhere I would rather be, like Robin Morse's "Acting the Song" class, and some that made me think I would rather be anywhere else. It was difficult to transition back into school, and I missed being in *Fiddler* more than I could have imagined. It felt like there was a piece of me missing.

Fiddler was extended at the National Yiddish Theatre Folksbiene through the end of the year, which was a huge and exciting success. I was thrilled for the show, and everyone involved, and also overjoyed that I would be able to see it as an audience member. Seeing

Fiddler on the Roof in Yiddish from the audience for the first time was one of the most mind-blowingly magical experiences. I was completely captivated by the beautiful storytelling and moved beyond words. All of my favorite parts to watch from the wings were a million times better from the audience. I loved it so much that I ended up seeing it four times. Meanwhile, I texted, called, and had video chats with my *Fiddler* friends frequently, and they came to visit me at school many times. They invited me to events too and made clear that I was still a part of the family, even though I had left. When the cast celebrated Jodi and Rachel's birthdays, I hurried down to meet them after class, and when they ran the 5K for Broadway Cares, I made posters with Raquel and went to cheer them on. One of my favorite memories was getting a random text from Raquel asking if I wanted to come watch the cast sing at Broadway Sessions, and racing down after school in my sweaty dance clothes to watch everyone sing. They ended up making me go onstage too, and I embarrassingly sang "Tomorrow" from *Annie*, with a sweatshirt tied around my waist over my ripped leggings. I got to hang out with Maya Jacobson, the wonderful woman who took over the role of Beylke, and I even got to ride back uptown with Jodi when the night was over. Though I climbed into bed at two in the morning and knew I would barely get six hours of sleep before another full day of school, it was the best night I had had in a while.

In November, my *Fiddler* friends told me that they

found out the show was going to transfer to a midtown Off-Broadway location. Everyone was excited, but they were told that the casting had not been decided yet, so no one knew what was going to

happen, or who was going to transfer with the show. The next day, I got out of the shower to find that I had a missed call. I was getting ready to go watch Rachel and Adam sing at a concert in honor of Marin Mazzie, when I listened to a voicemail from Jamibeth Margolis, the casting director from *Fiddler*, asking me to give her a call back as soon as possible. I immediately called her, and she told me that Joel and the creative team wanted me to come back to the show for the transfer to Stage 42. I was basically stunned into silence; she hung up the phone to give me some time to think about it. In my wildest dreams I had imagined this happening, and I couldn't believe it was real. I started sobbing into my sopping hair and called my mother to tell her. When she picked up the phone, I said, in complete hysterics, "Mama, Jamibeth called and they want me back in the show, and I'm not allowed to tell anyone yet, and I have to leave for this concert in an hour, and I'm in my bathrobe, and I forgot to eat dinner, and I can't stop crying, and I need to decide what I'm going to do… and I just have to do it, I just have to!"

I was a mess, struggling to talk to my mom on the phone about the possibility of me returning to the show, frantically trying to put on makeup with shaky hands to get ready for the concert, jumping up and down with excitement, and bursting into sobbing fits. She told me to breathe and go make myself some dinner first, which I did, and then we calmly talked it through. Like in the last decision I had to make about being at school or being in *Fiddler*, my family supported me either way. I was halfway through my junior year at that point, so it still seemed like an impossible choice to make. The difference this time was that from the minute Jamibeth asked me if I could come back to the show, I wanted to scream, "YES!" My heart, my brain, and my gut were all in agreement. Everyone I called for advice had similar reactions to the last time: some people told me I had to stay at school, other people told me I had to go with the show, and everyone told me that I would be fine either way. This time, though, before the conversation was over, whoever I was talking to would say something along the lines of, "It seems like you know what you're going to do."

That night, I went to watch Rachel and Adam in the concert, with Raquel, Jen, and James. I had a huge secret bursting inside me, and I prayed that no one would talk about the transfer. Right before the show started, Raquel turned to me and said, "I wonder if, for the transfer, they are thinking of replacing me with a real child, or someone famous." My heart started beating unreasonably fast, and I replied, "No way, that'd be crazy! I wouldn't even worry about it, if I were you." Not being able to tell anyone in the cast or at school was absolute torture. I had to inform the head of my program that I would be taking a leave of absence to do the show, but I wasn't even allowed to tell my teachers. It was an extremely difficult secret to have for the last month of school, as I snuck to fill out forms and have meetings with college administrators between classes, but also an amazing one, as I looked up pictures of Stage 42 with

curiosity and excitement. I kept a little post-it beside my bed with the quote: "You must give up the life you had planned in order to have the life that is waiting for you."

Meanwhile, I was missing a couple days of school for two different *Fiddler* events — the Cast Album recording, and a photo shoot for the transfer. Both were unbelievably exciting, and though I had to keep them on the down-low at school, I had all of my *Fiddler* family to kvell about them with me. On November 29th, 2018, we made the original cast recording; it was a magnificent dream-day. The Manhattan Center, where we recorded, was a huge, beautiful space; I couldn't stop looking at the ceiling all day. The original cast, including me, came back to sing our original parts. Every member of the current cast was also there, at least singing in the ensemble. It was a joyful combination of company. It was my first time seeing Joel, since I left the show, and he knew that I was secretly coming back, so when he saw me that day he pushed past everyone, wrapped me up in a huge hug, and exclaimed, "There *is* a god!" We recorded on a big stage, standing all together as one big shtetl. When we weren't in the song that was being recorded, we got to watch from the balcony, which was fantastic. I got to stand next to Jodi, the incredibly talented Frume Sore, as she fiercely belted "The Dream," which made my heart explode with joy. Then, before we sang "Matchmaker," the five of us sisters got in a big group huddle and had a special moment together. Singing "Matchmaker" for the first time in months with Rachel, Stephanie, Rosie, and Raquel, felt like coming home. The next day I watched the documentary on the making of the original cast album of *Company,* still reveling in the warmth of the day, and the amazing milestone of recording my first cast album.

Weeks later, I went to my first ever photoshoot with the one and only Matthew Murphy. They were getting a photo of Tevye and his daughters as artwork for the transfer to Stage 42. Steven, Rachel, Stephanie, Rosie, Raquel and I took a car to the studio together, with Tim Peters who helped us all get into costume and do our makeup. Matthew Murphy started with solo shots of just Steven, while the daughters all sat on the couch and watched in awe. There were worlds in Steven's eyes, and every single one of the pictures was coming out so beautifully. He added the daughters into the picture, one by one, and then he did a bunch of shots of all five of us circling around Steven. It was like a game of musical chairs — we walked around Steven, and when Matthew Murphy called "Stop," we all moved in to hug Steven from wherever we were. It was so much fun. When Joel arrived at the photo shoot, he snuck an extra shmata around his head and jumped in the picture, cuddling up to Steven like Tevye's sixth daughter. We all laughed hysterically, and the delight and wonder in our faces was exactly what Matthew Murphy needed for the photo. After the photo shoot, Joel took a car with us all back to the theatre, where everyone except for me had an evening show. The five of us girls went out to dinner and the mall for a joyful night of sisterly bonding, and then they got me a ticket to stay and watch the show. It was an incredible way to end an incredible day.

On the last day of my school semester, the cast list for the transfer was finally announced. I told my friends and my teachers that I was taking a year off of school to be in *Fiddler on the Roof in Yiddish* at Stage 42, and wouldn't be coming back after winter break. Everyone congratulated me, and some of my best friends and classmates cried because they were going to miss me. I got long hugs and goodbyes from everyone, and promises that they would come see the show. As I walked out the doors of Manhattan School of Music, I let out the deepest breath of the secret I had been keeping. I suddenly felt ten pounds lighter. Then it hit me — the realization that I had no idea what was going to happen next. I ran to my favorite park, climbed a tree, and started to worry about my future for the first time. I thought, *what am I going to do for a month until rehearsals start? What if the show closes after a week? What if they fire me? What if I never go back to school again? Am I ready to be in the real world? What if I regret this decision? What if I become terribly unhappy?* I texted Rachel, and she told me to listen to "Move On" from *Sunday in the Park with George*. I took a deep breath and then took a long walk to Stage 42. I stared up at my new home with wonder, listening to the wise words of Steven Sondheim: "Stop worrying where you're going — move on. If you can know where you're going, you've gone. Just keep moving on."

* * *

Grant Richards

Role: Ensemble

The first time I walked into the new theatre I was immediately filled with joy. I am so happy that the show transferred to a house size it deserves so this wonderful story can continue to be shared. The first few times I was watching it I was a little worried because the space is so much larger than downtown, but it all translates so beautifully. The nuances and the emotional vulnerability of it carries through. The intimacy, simplicity, intention, and emotional integrity of what Joel created just grows with the space. I immediately felt that when I was coming back home into the show. My ultimate favorite part of the show is "Tradition." I feel like there is not another musical theatre number in the world that can compare to that song. It's an eleven o'clock number at the start of the show. The drums come in, and we come out of the wings with such energy and unity that the audience can't help but viscerally react. We are introduced as one big village. You feel the home, the heart, and the drive, and you immediately know what the show is about. There's also something I love about all of the cast members being onstage in the wedding. I get to hold one of the poles for the chuppah in the wedding scene, and there's a nice breath of light air and silence as the chuppah gets billowed. It's a moment of stillness with the entire cast in the first act, and it's become one of my favorite parts.

The cast recording was a beautiful experience. It's so rare what we are doing. It's amazing that we are telling this story in the language it was meant to be told in. Putting it on a cast recording that will be around forever is something that was so needed. I don't think there was ever a question whether it should be recorded and looked back on in twenty years as an important part of theatre history or not. It was a crazy whirlwind of a day. We had orchestra members, technicians, producers, cast members, creatives, stage managers, and people that we didn't even know were involved just coming together for the monumental occasion. We were in this huge ballroom and recording on a big stage, and when we weren't recording, we could watch the people who were. Everyone wanted to watch and be there to see it all, because everyone has such a piece of heart in it. Just having been in the room when Stephanie Lynne Mason and Drew Seigla recorded their duet, or when Steven Skybell yelled "Traditsye!" fifty-plus times is so special. For everyone to be able to stand there in the group numbers with their own microphone and look around and see each other was beautiful. Most cast recordings are done through individual tracking or individual booths or studios, so to all be in one room was really fantastic. It was perfect for our shtetl. There are months or years of sweat and tears in so many performances that live in cast recordings. It is really like a memory box of a show. It has so much life. Many people have put their heart and soul and effort into making this show happen and telling this story every night.

From the bottle dancers dripping sweat twice a day and destroying themselves to portray the original Jerome Robbins' vision, to Steven Skybell who goes out and constantly gives the most remarkable performance as Tevye. Everyone leaves their heart on the stage and is so invested that by the time of the exodus there normally isn't a dry eye in the audience or onstage.

* * *

Tim Peters

Star Dresser | Backup Wardrobe Supervisor

Working on this show has been such a rollercoaster. I joined the wardrobe team thinking that *Fiddler* was going to have a short run; my friend had asked me to take over for her, and I thought a month and a half at *Fiddler* sounded like a great little stint before I went back to my restaurant job. Slowly I became a part of this shtetl and realized how much I wanted to be here, even through the crazy weeks. It's fun to look back and see what we have accomplished as a team, and I've grown so much as a person here.

I am the lead/star dresser, and I swing up as the wardrobe supervisor when Sarah Dixie is out. On a typical day, I come to the theatre two hours before the show starts to get the laundry started. Depending on how much turnover we got done the night before, we will either get time to relax and hang out while the laundry runs, or we'll be distributing costume pieces to the dressing rooms. During the show I work with the three-star ladies of the show: Jennifer Babiak, Jackie Hoffman, and Rachel Zatcoff, who share a dressing room. I have little moments of changing them throughout the show, until we get to "The Dream." Then, it gets very hectic. When we get new swings in the costume department, it's always so funny to introduce them to the "The Dream" as the most stressful fifteen minutes of the show. During tech week, I remember getting a pimple the day after we tech-ed "The Dream" and saying, "Oh yeah, that's from that fifteen minutes of the show."

Those fifteen minutes start with a "joke circle" with Jodi Snyder, Evan Mayer, Rachel Zatcoff, Ben Liebert, and whoever else is available to join. My joke is that I never have a joke to contribute. Then I get Jodi into the Frume Sore dress and get Evan and Jodi ready to go on in "The Dream." When they go on, we have three minutes of waiting around, because there is nothing we can do while they are onstage. As soon as they run off, I catch the dress, and we quickly help Jodi out of it, making sure the wig stays on her as she leaves the dress. Then I immediately start getting Evan ready to be the bagel seller in the very next scene, "Tailor Shop 1," with Sarah. After Evan is all set, I run to the star ladies' dressing room. I get Jackie into her wedding blazer and pashmina, and by the time I'm done with that, Jen runs into the room and I get her into her wedding outfit. She takes off her garment from "The Dream" and I hand her the black blouse to put on. Then I button the back, put on the collar, and get her into her wig and vail. One of our traditions is that I tell Jen to have a good wedding before I leave, and then I run back to stage left to help Cameron Johnson get ready for the wedding scene. He hands me his red barrette, I give him his mustache, and then I put him in the black sweater. Then I get to breathe, because all of the changes in those fifteen minutes are done. After that, the wedding scene starts, and the wardrobe team plays "clean up." I hang up the Frume dress, spray it down, pre-set the red pashmina for Rosie Jo Neddy, and clean up anything else from the crazy fifteen minutes of making a mess. The second act is more relaxed and focused on folding laundry and preparing for the next show.

My favorite costume is Frume Sore's dress. I hate that dress, but I love that dress; I've worked with it so much I really understand it now. I feel the same way about Jackie's orange pashmina. They took so long to figure out, and to be comfortable with, but now I really know them like the back of my hand.

Being down in Battery Park for the summer, during the original run, was such a blast. We always went out for drinks or food on the pier after shows together. There was one time my dad and brother visited me, and we went to Ellis Island in the morning, and then they got to watch *Fiddler* that night while I worked backstage. It was such a surreal day to remember where we work, and what story we are telling with *Fiddler*. Even just walking by the Statue of Liberty was always a nice little refresher of how important it was to get to work there. Downtown, I always used to take naps on the bundles that everyone carries for the "Exodus" scene, because they were just in a huge pile on the ground backstage. We were constantly snacking, mostly on cheese-its.

I've picked up some Yiddish, like always asking "Vos?" when people talk to me instead of asking

"What?" I have a couple phrases that I like to say during the show too, like before Jackie enters the scene with the little boys in Act Two, I say, "Golde, bisht in shtub?" which means, "Golde, are you home?" There was one time I was singing "Miracle of Miracles" backstage but didn't really know the words. I said, "Dos is a mesgeven" and Mikhl Yashinsky turned to me and asked, "Oh, did you mean to make that joke?"

I said, "No, I don't really know the words." He said, "Oh, you just said 'mesgeven,' which means 'corpse,' instead of 'nesgeven,' which means miracle!" Then I started using the word 'mesgeven' all the time, which was cool because it is a Yiddish word that isn't in the show. It will definitely be weird, down the line, to not hear Yiddish all the time. It makes me think of how the high school that I went to was a deaf magnet school, so we had a lot of students who were deaf and hard of hearing. I would constantly see ASL, but now I never see it because it's not as saturated.

Being at the theatre on my birthday and celebrating with the company made me remember why I come to work every day. These are my people. I run around on crazy days, but then I get to relax and be here with the people that I love. We are such a family, and it shows in all of the little moments. Last week, Kayleen Seidl made her debut going on for Hodl, and we all were watching her from the wings. Anytime someone makes their understudy debut the whole cast and crew is there to watch. We all support each other and want to be there for everyone. Rachel Calter, the assistant stage manager, has seen me at the most stressed I have ever been, running around backstage downtown. It's nice being around people who have seen me in very heightened parts of my life that I didn't expect to experience here.

The photo shoot for the transfer was an amazing experience. I was so stressed out, thinking, *do I have everything? Please don't let me have forgotten anything at the theatre.* It was all I was thinking about during the car ride there, and when we got there and the girls were putting on their costumes, I was able to chill out and actually take in this wonderful experience. Getting to be there with Joel to watch the photos being taken for our commercial transfer was just so surreal; it was a "pinch me" moment.

When we moved uptown to Stage 42, we got to be in the theatre a week before the cast. We set up and made the space look nice for everyone and turned it into the home where we are going to spend hopefully a very long time. I don't think I will fully realize until fifteen years down the line what this show has really been to me, but I'm getting a taste of the fact that this is affecting my life in a way that I never would have expected.

* * *

Jordan Porch

A2 | Backup Mixer

Fiddler has been my third Yiddish show, so it has been really great delving into the Yiddish language more. This time, I actually took to learning the language: reading a textbook and having support from Yiddishist friends. Learning more Yiddish has been very informative in how I work when I'm mixing the show, although I'm usually the A2, and it also afforded me the opportunity to learn and run the supertitles track. It's been new and interesting for me to expand on the experience I had a couple years ago with the National Yiddish Theatre Folksbiene. My first experience with the Folksbiene happened out of nowhere and saved me from working in a hotel, whereas *Fiddler* caught me in my senior year of college. I really think this was meant to be because it was relatively easy for me to juggle school and work on this. It's also easier to do difficult things when you really want to do them. I really wanted this to work out, so I had to make sacrifices, cover my bases, and be upfront about my availability. I also knew that I had to do one last production at school, so I got a sub and made sure to check up on them the whole time leading up to it. I got very lucky with my schedule, and it wasn't as hard as it could have been.

I am the A2/backup mixer on *Fiddler*, which means I'm usually preparing the wireless microphones and maintaining them, working backstage to help the actors get into microphones, taping their mics on, and checking everyone's mic placement. A typical day is spent backstage listening to the show and being able to troubleshoot things as they happen while the A1 is able to focus on mixing the show. I also watch the quick changes and other moments to prevent anything from going wrong with the microphones.

It feels more relaxed in certain ways working at Stage 42 than it did downtown at the museum because we have the protections of the union, which has been really nice and great to learn about. My school has a union house, so I've worked with union stagehands a lot, but being under those same protections now is very great. When we were down at the museum, I had my first experience with a production that had a threat of transferring, and that actually added a lot of stress into the job. Trying to do your normal, day-to-day job while having the burden of wondering whether or not you will get to transfer with the show, which a lot of people didn't, was not easy. Now that we transferred to Stage 42, we are just chilling and hoping that we sell a lot of tickets. I'm really happy about everything that has happened so far, and to have been doing this for a year is more than I could've hoped for. Right now, we are supposed to run until January, so I'm just hoping for that to happen. My favorite part about working here is the people I get to see every day. It's almost the same as it was for me at school; there is a security of knowing everyone is genuinely happy to be here, doing whatever their job is.

I also love the Yiddish aspect, because it's more special than just a normal revival of a musical, and we're all here learning new things every day.

One of my proudest moments from this experience was attending the Easter Bonnet Competition for Broadway Cares, in which I was not a participant but really enjoyed seeing everyone up there doing an original Yiddish work based on existing musical theatre history. The moment it ended and I heard the audience roaring, and so surprised by what they just saw, was a moment of beaming pride for me, having worked in the Yiddish theatre for a few years now. I love everyone's reception of it, and I am just hoping that it continues to sell more tickets.

* * *

Motl Didner

Associate Director | Yiddish Coach | Supertitle Designer

I've been with the National Yiddish Theatre Folksbiene since 2003, and our audiences are very free with their suggestions; from my earliest memories of working here, I remember people saying we should do *Fiddler on the Roof* in Yiddish. The cast recording of the Israeli production of *Fidler Afn Dakh,* translated by Shraga Friedman in 1965, circulated very widely in the American Yiddishist community. The songs from *Fiddler* in Yiddish were recorded by American artists like Jan Peerce and often were included in Yiddish concerts. There were Yiddish *Fiddler* productions done in various translations in Bucharest, Warsaw, and Montreal, but never in the United States. It was an obvious choice, but there were certain realities that made it easier said than done. It was a much bigger show than we had ever taken on: when I began, the biggest shows we had done only involved twelve to fifteen people including the orchestra. *Fiddler* requires a minimum of twenty-five actors plus an orchestra. There had also never been an Off-Broadway production of *Fiddler* in New York. There was no precedent for the authors to grant the right for anything smaller than a Broadway production, and somebody always held the option for the rights to the next Broadway revival.

We often incorporated songs from *Fiddler* in Yiddish in our annual gala concerts. There were three or four performances where we had Theodore Bikel and Fyvush Finkel, who both had enormously long careers with *Fiddler*, singing the Yiddish version of "To Life" along with the Tevye and Leyzer-Volf scene which leads into the song. We also had Sheldon Harnick singing "Do You Love Me" a few times at our galas, the most memorable being his duet with Andrea Martin who blanked on the words and improvised by singing,

"I forgot the lyrics even though I'm standing next to the lyricist!"

For the fiftieth anniversary of *Fiddler* in 2014, the Folksbiene's gala at Town Hall was the definitive *Fiddler* reunion concert. We had original cast members, stars from the film, and stars from the Broadway revivals over the years. It was an enormous gathering of *Fiddler* alumni, and it set us on a course to begin talking very seriously about doing *Fidler Afn Dakh*. We had to wait for the most recent revival of *Fiddler on the Roof* on Broadway to run its course, and when the show closed, we made serious inquiries to obtain the rights. We found the sweet spot before the next company could option the rights, and that was the "miracle of miracles" for us. We announced that we were going to do *Fidler Afn Dakh* in December of 2017 at a gala where we were honoring Jerry Zaks. The audience was a "Who's Who"of Broadway, and the room exploded with energy when we made the announcement. Word spread very quickly among the theatre community.

We didn't have a director booked yet, but we had already established a relationship with Joel Grey, having honored him at a gala in 2013. More recently, Joel participated in a marathon reading of Elie Wiesel's *Night*, after Elie Wiesel passed away in 2016. Originally, we thought of Joel for the role of Tevye. It was Hal Prince, whom Zalmen Mlotek called about the project, who suggested Joel as the director. Joel accepted the offer fairly quickly, but there was still a little bit of convincing left to do around the project. In February of 2018, we put together a table read. It was very top secret, because we hadn't announced anything publicly yet — we had to make sure that it was really going to work. Of the eight or nine people who participated in that table read, Adam Shapiro and Stephanie Lynne Mason ended up in the production. Zalmen read and played the songs, and I read for the character Motl. We were sitting in a beautiful board room at the Museum of Jewish Heritage with a sweeping view of the harbor, Ellis Island, and the Statue of Liberty. It moved all of us, including Joel, and at that point there was no doubt about it — we were all onboard.

The casting process was amazing. When I first started working at the Folksbiene, we had maybe a couple hundred people who would submit themselves to audition for our productions. By the time of our *Fiddler* auditions, our reputation was growing after our string of hits with *The Golden Bride* and *Amerike the Golden Land*, and we had our well-connected casting director Jamibeth Margolis. The prospect of doing *Fiddler* with Joel Grey as the director took it to a completely new level, and we were amazed by the turnout. We had twenty-five hundred people submit themselves, of which we saw seven hundred people. To choose a cast of twenty-six from seven hundred people meant that we really got the best of the best.

Cast cohesion is usually pretty amazing with

Folksbiene shows, because I think there is a shared experience of delving into a show that is not in your language. There is something about it that bonds people, because they are going through something a lot more difficult than a standard rehearsal for a show. I've never seen anything quite like the cohesion in this cast, though — it is truly striking. It's more than a shtetl, it's a real family. It's a beautiful thing to see, and I love the humor and comradery backstage that started all the way downtown at the Folksbiene and still continues at Stage 42. Everyone is having a genuinely good time.

Early on, there was a question of how long the show was going to run. I said, "This is *Fiddler,* it's Joel Grey, and it's a great cast. It's going to run six months." There was still a lot of worry around it because it was a Yiddish show, so we announced a six-week run. Then it kept extending again and again following the audience demand. I could not have imagined that we would be here at Stage 42 — that was an unprecedented and amazing thing to happen. The fact that we are still here, and that we have recorded a cast album, is incredible. To think that in 2019 a Yiddish production is going to run in New York for a minimum of eighteen months is crazy — *meshuggah.*

Part Eleven
Schlep

Sammy

Role: Beylke

On the first day of rehearsal for the transfer to Stage 42, which was January 29th, 2019, I woke up early to curl my hair, and put on my favorite blue shirt with ruffles on the sleeves. I bounced in my seat on the thirty-minute subway ride to midtown, proudly wearing my Fiddler bracelet from our opening night, along with my biggest smile of excitement. I had practiced my track over and over again, worrying that I would fall behind in rehearsal since I had not been with the company for many months, and was giddy to start. Early as usual, I signed in at Ripley Grier Studios, where we were going to have one week of rehearsal before moving to the theatre to tech and open the show. The first day of rehearsal was like a family reunion — we squeezed each other upon arrival and buzzed around the room in a familiar chaos. Everyone gave extra hugs to Evan Mayer, Kayleen Seidl, Mikhl Yashinsky, Lisa Fishman, and me, because we were returning from not having been in the show for a while. Being with everyone again

191

was so joyful. We met our new lead producers, Hal Luftig and Jana Robbins, along with a lot of new members of the production and marketing teams. There were introductions and speeches, and then Joel sang the same song he sang on opening night, "When I Was Eight Days Old." We all knew the words at that point, because he sang it on every remarkable occasion, so some people sang along, laughing delightedly. There was a miniature model of the new stage, with a cut-out picture of Steven Skybell as Tevye in it, a sizable spread of bagels and fruit, and a table with brand new scripts for each of us. We mingled and ate our bagels happily, and Connor Santos, our new social media coordinator, took a video of Rachel and me dancing around with our new scripts.

The production team and marketers left after the initial mingling and introductions, but before we started the rehearsal, we had an Actors' Equity Association meeting. There were several of us about to get our Equity cards, which was extremely exciting for me and a huge accomplishment for all of us. An Equity representative came to talk to us and teach us a little bit about the rights and responsibilities that come with joining the union. I could barely keep up with the information she was spewing, and when she gave us forms to fill out, I more or less copied off of Raquel's paper. Nonetheless, joining the union brought me a special kind of warmth. I was making a career out of my passion and joining a community of incredible artists and humans. It felt like someone was shaking my hand

and saying, "You want to be an actress? Okay! Welcome to the family!" After the Equity meeting, the room was left to the directors, stage managers, and cast: then, the real rehearsal process began.

The week of rehearsal at Ripley for the transfer packed almost as many surprises, challenges, lessons, and emotions as the three weeks of rehearsal we had downtown for the original run. We started with a vocal session, in which Zalmen informed us that all of the supertitles for the musical numbers were going to drastically change. Downtown, the supertitles displayed a direct translation of the Yiddish lyrics we were singing. These lyrics were from the original translation of Shraga Friedman, which were not an exact translation of the original Sheldon Harnick lyrics in most cases, in order to maintain the musicality and rhyme scheme. Because of these differences, Zalmen and Motl Didner had made some lyric changes for the transfer, including most of "Miracle of Miracles." On top of that, instead of displaying the direct translation of our Yiddish lyrics on the supertitles, they were going to show the original *Fiddler on the Roof* lyrics. For us, this meant that we would sometimes sing things like "Don't send us to the wedding canopy like sheep to meet a horrible end," while the audience read, "Up to this minute I misunderstood that I could get stuck for good." Zalmen asked us if we had any questions, and everyone immediately started flipping through their scripts to find discrepancies. We eventually came to the conclusion that they had already reached, which was that none of the lyrics were so different that our acting choices wouldn't make sense. The only big change for me was that the "Any day now" lyrics in the "lessons with Perchik" scene in Act One, Scene Six were completely different. This was problematic because during the scene we acted out the words with little choreographed arm motions, so Motl helped us change the movements to be just vague enough to make sense with what we were saying as well as what was being projected. Meanwhile, Ben Liebert, the incredible mensch that he is, learned the completely new lyrics for "Miracle of Miracles." The rest of the music rehearsal, which I spent contently seated between Rachel and Raquel, was wonderful. Singing "Tradition" together again felt like a real celebration of love and familial pride, because it was one big family reunion. When we sang "Sabbath Prayer," Jennifer Babiak turned around in her chair to look at all of the daughters, as she looks at us in the scene. When she looked at me, I couldn't hold back my tears, feeling the warmth of the beautiful music and her shining eyes. I remember making eye contact with Kayleen during "Sunrise, Sunset" and thinking, through our earsplitting grins, how we must both be feeling the same immense amount of gratitude to be back.

When we began our choreography rehearsal, Staś told us that he wanted to try something new for the beginning of "Tradition." Instead of stomping on from the wings in one big, unified line, he wanted us all trickling in from different sides of the stage while doing some simple, pedestrian business. He assigned different crosses and walking patterns for people, and had different groups or couples conversing in the background of Tevye's opening dialogue. There were even baskets and props added for people to use in the background crosses. It felt horribly distracting and the entire cast hated it immediately. Gone was our prideful, powerful, unified entrance; we were wandering around the stage with little motivation or purpose. There was nothing about it that aptly represented the shtetl we were introducing to the audience, or the special, moving story we were telling. We were constantly denouncing it to each other and making bets on when it would be changed back to the original choreography. To our dismay, it lasted and developed through the whole week at Ripley Grier Studios.

During the week, we touched on all of the musical numbers, but seemed to spend the most amount of time working on "Tradition," and the "Khavelah Ballet." We practiced the "Khavelah Ballet" so many times that we started jokingly and exhaustedly referring to it as "khavalabala." We also worked on "Matchmaker," and added some of my current favorite parts to it. Staś had seen us get into a sisterly huddle at the cast recording before singing "Matchmaker," and told us that it inspired him, so he added a sisterly huddle into the number, right before the end, where we all came together to squeeze each other for a minute. In addition to that, the "glasses bit" was added to the number, which is one of my favorite parts to do. When Rachel, as Tsaytl, starts to imitate Yente in the song, she comes over to me, snatches the glasses off my face, and puts them on to impersonate Yente. Then I get to blindly stumble around until Tsaytl takes off the glasses, and I run to get them back. I was so excited about the new bit because it was a fun acting challenge, it was a hilarious moment between Rachel and me, and it created a new sisterly dynamic between Tsaytl and Beylke that was very real and playable. As ready and willing as I was to do it, I somehow kept forgetting to get my glasses back from Tsaytl at the end. We ran it a few times, and Rachel patiently waited with my glasses in her hand until I realized I was supposed to run and grab them from her. During the third time we ran it, by the time I ran up to her to get the glasses, I was so late that she decided to just throw them into the basket of laundry. I quickly followed the glasses through the air, dug them out of the laundry, slammed them on my face, and ran back to my spot. The whole room was cracking up with laughter at the hilarious moment during the song, and I was never late again.

One of my favorite parts of that rehearsal week was watching the development of my two favorite scenes: Act One, Scene Six, when Tsaytl tells Tevye that she can't marry Leyzer-Volf, and "Do You Love Me." They were my favorite scenes to watch downtown, and they somehow became even more magnificent uptown. With

Joel's direction, and Steven, Jen, Rachel, and Ben's incredible acting, the scenes transcended their original structure, and took on a life of their own. I was able to watch those four beautiful actors take crazy, vulnerable leaps, which was the most awe-inspiring experience. I remember sitting in the front of the room, hugging my knees to my chest, and tearing up while watching Rachel do scene 1.6 in front of everyone for the first time in Ripley. Joel had given her a new direction to allow herself to sob through the entire beginning of the scene, and she used it in the most beautiful way. It was absolutely breathtaking, and the way it affected her scene partners and the rest of the scene was extremely moving. Moments like that are why I feel excited to go to the theatre every day.

* * *

Cameron Johnson

Role: Fyedke

During the rehearsal process for the re-mounting of *Fiddler* at Stage 42, our choreographer Staś Kmieć, turned to me and said, "Cam, you know how you lift Rosie during the 'Khavelah Ballet'? I think instead of lifting her cradle style and carrying her around, I want you to lift her… up over your head. With straight arms. And then twist her around and put her down on the other side." I said okay, and we tried it. It didn't really work though, because something was wrong leverage-wise. We did it again and it still didn't work. So naturally we did it twenty more times until I said, "OOH. My back." I threw it out. The next day I woke up with terrible pain. My lower back, which is usually concave, was convex and I could barely move. I wore a brace and had to cancel some things. This was right before opening night. I couldn't carry Rosie, I just had to walk her offstage, and I couldn't jump off the table in "L'Chaim" after I sang my long note. It was a really hard time. It was the opening and the press was coming to the other shows that week, and I could barely move. I was being super mindful not to twist my torso at all, and I felt like I was just waiting for my back to break. It was about six weeks before I could do my normal lift with Rosie, which is the only version of the lift we ever do now.

I love that I have a friendship with Joel Grey now. Every time I see him it's just so nice and he's happy to see me, and that just makes me feel really good. I have video proof that we are friends. When he was singing "Willkommen" to raise money for Broadway Cares, he came over to me and gave me that little punch on the chin that you give to your friends. I have it on video so that's my evidence. Also, in the past three months, Ben Liebert and I have played twenty-nine tournaments of cribbage. A tournament is the first to seven games, so some tournaments are thirteen games. We're kindred spirits. We play every minute that we are both offstage.

I'm taking a break from cribbage to do this interview right now. My favorite onstage moment is "L'Chaim." There is a big bar scene where I stand on a table to interrupt the song by singing a very long and high note. I just hold it for as long as I wish and then I come down and the moment is mine. I change the atmosphere of the scene. At the table during the bar scene, we are actually playing cards too. I play cribbage backstage and crazy eights onstage. We call crazy eights "Meshuggeneh Okht," though.

Outside of *Fiddler* I teach fitness classes, often very early in the morning, and I have a wife and a toddler. That means that I have about thirty minutes of free time in every given week, aside from when I'm playing cribbage. Having a toddler is demanding timewise, but it's not like there's anything I would rather do. So it's hard, but good.

* * *

Joanne Borts

Role: Sheyndl | Golde, Yente, Frume Sore Understudy

I met Zalmen Mlotek, our *Fiddler* musical director, when I was a little kid, back when I started going to mitlshul in the Village on Bank Street. Mitlshul was the upper level of the Arbeter Ring Shule, kind of the

Yiddish version of "Hebrew School." I met a bunch of really cool and talented kids there, who all had European-born parents and spoke Yiddish at home. Zalmen was our singing teacher at mitlshul. He was an amazing piano player and musician, and all the cool kids already knew him from their summers at Camp Hemshekh. He could play just about anything by ear, and he could change keys in two seconds flat, which was a real bonus for our adolescent voices. It was the first time I remember kids calling teachers by their first names, too, so he was just "Zalmen." At the time, Zalmen was also musical directing lots of Yiddish concerts all over the city, and he was always schlepping our class to perform at lots of different venues, including the Waldorf Astoria and Avery Fisher Hall. It was a pretty big deal, but I'm sure I didn't realize it at the time. I was that 'little kid with a big voice', so he threw all of these interesting Yiddish songs in front of me and my pals. We would sing concerts with many of the great stars of the Yiddish theatre, like Mina Bern, Ben Bonus, Claire Barry from the Barry Sisters, Emil Gorovets, and even Jan Peerce. Zalmen would try to explain, "This is someone really important! Don't you understand what it means to be doing a concert with them?" I was wide-eyed and really naive, and I definitely didn't know who anyone was, so my parents eventually had to fill me in.

After mitlshul and through high school and university, I continued to work on a bunch of programs with Zalmen, including the annual Arbeter Ring Third

Seder, often with many of those same artists who remembered me as the 'little kid with the big voice'. I had just graduated from college when Zalmen gave me a call and said he needed me to perform a couple of 'dates' for a new show he'd co-written with his cousin, Moishe Rosenfeld, called *The Golden Land.* My *Golden Land* experience lasted almost four years, after which I was invited to be part of Zalmen and Moishe's subsequent projects, *On Second Avenue* and *Those Were the Days,* which I was able to intersperse with other awesome theatre gigs, including the 1990 Broadway revival of *Fiddler on the Roof* with Topol. When we performed the first iteration of *Those Were the Days*, at the Walnut Street Theatre in Philadelphia, I sang a song that we had picked off of an old record that Zalmen had listened to back in the 1960s — "Shadkhnte, Shadkhnte" which is "Matchmaker, Matchmaker" from *Fiddler on the Roof,* translated into Yiddish by Shraga Friedman. Yiddish *Fiddler* was already floating in the ether.

A few years later Zalmen and I co-created a new project for the Workmen's Circle Convention called "Kids & Yiddish." He knew I would be the perfect fit. Not only did Zalmen remember that 'little kid with the big voice' but he knew that preserving and performing Yiddish was my ongoing passion. For so many years, Yiddish had had a reputation as old-fashioned, 'immigrant-y' and the language parents would speak when they were trying to keep secrets from the kids. But for me, Yiddish is the language of teenage rebellion, first kisses, social justice, lifelong friendships — *khavershaft,* and continuation — *hemshekh.* My goal has always been to teach Yiddish to kids, so their parents won't understand them!

When the Folksbiene theatre decided to produce *Fidler Afn Dakh,* it seemed like another perfect fit. From my very first audition with Joel Grey, it was clear that this production was going to be new and different — and not just because of the translation. Joel had envisioned the show with fresh eyes and wanted to tell this familiar tale with a new voice. He made sure we steered clear of anything stereotypical or 'schticky', which allowed its truth and universality to emerge without creating a shtetl that was 'victimized.' Joel also made sure that the women in Tevye's life, his wife, Golde, and his five daughters, would illuminate the story in a way that I've never seen presented in any other production of *Fiddler.* For all our disparate familiarity with *Fiddler* or Yiddish, it felt as if the whole company entered our little shtetl of Anatevka as a community. Together, the cast re-learned how to tell Tevye's timeless story in an ancient language to a twenty-first century audience. More than any other gig I can remember, *Fidler Afn Dakh* is definitely an amalgam of the most important aspects of my artistic experience: a true marriage of my classic theatre life and my traditional Yiddish career. My Yiddish and English theatre worlds have officially collided, in the best of all possible ways. When Zalmen pulled me aside at an early

Yiddish Fiddler rehearsal and asked me to clarify some of the orchestra cues for the vignettes in "Traditsye" it felt as if we'd truly reached an "adult" place. Zalmen and I defer to each other on certain things and challenge each other on others, but we continue to work together as artists and equals. I look back on my life and realize how lucky I've been to have had so many incredible teachers and mentors.

I truly love working with this amazing Fiddler company. It's a privilege to be part of it. I love how all the actors, especially the young people in the cast, are so diligent about the Yiddish language and culture. This show has certainly proven that Yiddish is alive and well and living on 42nd Street and beyond. *Fidler Afn Dakh* is no longer a curiosity; Yiddish *Fiddler* is a phenomenon.

* * *

Lauren Thomas

Role: Der Fiddler

I've always been a huge fan of *Fiddler on the Roof* and wondered if I'd ever get to play The Fiddler professionally, but figured the opportunity would never arise since male dancers are typically cast in the role. When the EPA was announced for Yiddish Fiddler, I was tempted to audition, but then I saw they were really only looking for Yiddish speakers, so I decided not to go. A few weeks passed, and I saw on Actors Access that they were looking for the role of The Fiddler, and they listed that both men and women could apply. I got an appointment and was surprised when Jamibeth sent back pages of Yiddish for me to prepare in addition to the Fiddler theme for the audition. I listened to the clips Motl Didner made, over and over, and had them memorized when I went in the room. It felt like a huge accomplishment to get through the Yiddish in the audition room, and when I came out, the other actors were buzzing about how Joel Grey had been in the room. Of course, I knew of the legend Joel Grey but had no idea what he looked like. I was glad I waited until after the audition to google him to keep my nerves down in the room. For the callback, they told us to wear long skirts and shmatas, and I was so intrigued about what their vision for The Fiddler would be, and if I would be in a shmata on the roof, speaking Yiddish, if cast. The choreographer Staś Kmieć taught me the "fiddle-dance" in the room, and it was so exciting to dance it in a long skirt. They also had me play the Fiddler theme again but asked me to make each melodic line a different character or secret. After that callback, I wanted to be part of the production so badly, because it felt like they had such a fresh vision for what this show would be. Although I am more androgynous than I initially thought I'd be as The Fiddler from the audition experience, it feels really special to be a female Fiddler.

It's fun to get to bring a youthful, feminine energy to the character, especially in those moments when Tevye is trying to decide whether or not to follow tradition in the "Rebuttals". And in "Khavelah Ballet", I feel like the sixth sister as the daughters' circle around me.

To start a show that we thought was going to last for six weeks, and then be able to continue and see the growth of it is really special. Not only has our show evolved, but my character as well. Downtown, I started with no makeup, and I felt slightly distant from the action due to the shape of the stage. Uptown, I feel more integrated in the action, especially during the rebuttals, where I'm just an arm's reach away from Tevye. I'm also in the very top of act two, which makes me feel more part of Tevye's battle with Tradition. Our directors have been so wonderful about letting me ask questions and become more involved in developing this character. From the beginning, our musical director Zalmen Mlotek really encouraged me to play the melody with my own flare, and set up lessons for me with a Klezmer violinist, Jake Shulman-Ment, who helped me better understand the Klezmer feel. The Fiddler is not typically a real violinist. We worked together to figure out where I would play in the score and on stage in numbers such as "To Life," which originally The Fiddler character is not a part of.

I like that I'm an observer of everyone, but standing on the roof is pretty scary. After we had done the show for maybe fifty performances, our directors told me: "We need you to move more on the roof. You're reading stiff." I had to start moving my body more, standing on two stacked tables, which gets pretty nerve-wracking. It definitely makes Tevye's line about the balance of "Tradition" tangible for me. It's a powerful experience to get to start and end the show every day. The other night, there happened to be a lighting malfunction, and the house lights stayed up while I was coming on stage. I could see the audience finding their seats and shushing each other, and that we were about to enter the world of the play together. It's a cool moment, because I get to be part of that anticipation with them.

"To Life" is so fun and I'm really glad I get to be a part of it. Even though I'm just standing on a chair in the back, I love to watch those guys dance and I genuinely have so much fun every time I do that number. My favorite part is the wedding scene because I can see all of the little moments from where I am standing on stage right. When Perchik gets everyone to dance with each other, Joanne Borts and Steven Skybell have this cute moment where Joanne doesn't want to dance at all. Mikhl Yashinsky tries to get her to dance and she will hold on to the scarf to dance with him, but won't touch him. Then, when Steven joins their circle, he comes in and grabs her hand without her realizing and she has a moment of: *Oh my god! I'm touching a man!* Then they start laughing about it and it is so cute. It's such a well-formed moment which I don't think most people can see. There are so many moments like that, especially in the wedding scene when everyone is onstage. I wish someone could take a picture of that scene so we could see all of the vignettes.

Part Twelve
Mazel

Sammy

Role: Beylke

Matthew Murphy's picture of Tevye and the five daughters from the photo shoot went up on telephone booths and bus stops all around the city. It looked like I had a huge double chin in the photo, which made me look more like Robin Williams than a twenty-year-old girl. Nonetheless, it was still the most exciting thing ever. Moreover, the double-chin effect was merely a piece of Rosie Jo Neddy's hair that swept over my face. After just one week of rehearsal at Ripley Grier, we were off to Stage 42 to tech and open the show. On February 5th, 2019, we had our first day at Stage 42. Raquel, Jodi, and I got up early to have breakfast at Westway Diner and take pictures in front of the marquee before rehearsal. The marquee was gorgeous — glowing in yellow, with words, lights, and joyous pictures from *Fiddler*. We went through the official "Stage Door," and up a janky elevator with foam stars scattered randomly on the walls. When the elevator doors opened, the first thing we saw was the big poster from Joel that we had all signed downtown, that said: "Fiddish Spoken Here." We took in our new surroundings, settling in the fact that this was going to be our new home for hopefully a long time.

After passing a small kitchen and bathroom on our right, we entered what is known as the "green room." It was a big area right off of the stage left wings where there was a monitor set up that had a live view of the stage, so the actors could watch what was happening, and two big couches on either side for relaxing in. Next to the green room was our callboard: the big bulletin board where stage management posts our sign- in sheet, daily call times, news and information, signups for cast talkbacks and other events, and a "Yiddish quote of the day." By the callboard was a large water cooler, and then a long hallway that led straight to stage right, and branched to go down to the stage management office, wardrobe room, and the four dressing rooms. My dressing room station was between Raquel and Lauren Thomas, in front of a huge mirror that covered the whole upper wall. The wardrobe team had set up name tags for us, hooks to hold our masks for "The Dream" and any other accessories, as well as costume racks. We had a bathroom and shower, a mini fridge that Jackie Hoffman had gifted us downtown, and, of course, our Equity cot. It was super exciting and glamorous, but at the same time it looked like there could be creatures living in the couch cushions.

Sitting in the theatre for the first time, and seeing

the space we were going to perform in was thrilling. The wings were huge, lined with countless ropes and other unknown things, and the ceiling was high and beautiful; I felt like Alice in *Alice in Wonderland,* exploring the new backstage area. I loved every little nook and cranny I laid my eyes on, even the little ladder that hung above the stage left wing that I always looked up at, in fear of it falling on me. The audience was arranged with stadium seating, so it still felt like an intimate space even though it was bigger. Stage 42 was the perfect home for us to move into.

Tech week was more exhausting than I could've imagined. There were multiple days in a row where we had to be at the theatre for twelve hours straight, and we spent thirteen days at the theatre without even one day off. Luckily, on our first day of tech, the producers brought us frozen yogurt from Pinkberry to keep us in good spirits. To brighten our spirits even more, we started rehearsal with "Tradition," and immediately found out that we were changing it back to our original staging. There was a collective cheer throughout the cast, and we stepped onto Stage 42 for the first time together with the biggest smiles and proudest postures. We put all of our might and passion into the opening stomps, whispering to each other that we had to really "sell it" and make this version stick. We were extremely successful, of course; our beautiful, unified entrance stuck. Throughout tech week, we battled exhaustion with humor and familial moments. We danced around in the wings, played around with fun ad libs, and decorated our dressing room stations. One of the highlights was Steven Skybell taking silly, candid photos of everyone backstage. We got daily notes on acting, singing, dancing, and Yiddish, which we worked our hardest to adjust, and a lot of small changes were made.

One day we were running the pogrom at the end of the first act, and it was just Tevye's immediate family onstage listening to the offstage pogrom. Suddenly, Joel stood up from his seat in the theatre and yelled, "Gunshot!" Our tears from the scene immediately turned to laughter as we broke character at his hilarious outburst. Joel's idea carried through, and the next day we stood on the stage while Joel listened to options of gunshot sound effects. Somewhere in the process, eerie music was added into the offstage pogrom. We were told to turn and look around the whole theatre as the music played, as if we were hearing the offstage pogrom all around us. The music was unbelievably strange, and the concept seemed so ridiculous that none of us could get into it. It quickly got cut, but the gunshot stayed, followed by a piercing scream from Jodi Snyder offstage. It was very effective. At the end of tech week, we were all walking zombies — completely dead on our feet. When we finally got a day off, most of us did nothing but catch up on sleep.

On the day of our first preview, we were all overjoyed to see our new playbill. It was my first time being in a real, official playbill — the kind that every Broadway show uses. On top of that, I was thrilled to tears to see the picture from our photoshoot on the cover. My face, as double-chin-seeming as it was, was on a playbill. After the show I ran up and down the aisles of the theatre to collect all of the discarded playbills to take home with me. Of course, I later realized that I could have just asked for a stack of playbills, but this was much more fun. We had a little pizza party after the successful first preview, and when we went back to grab our belongings before going home, there was a ghost light on the stage. I had always loved hearing about the ghost lights at theatres, so seeing our very own ghost light made me beam from the inside out.

February 21st, 2019 was our opening night — it was an absolute dream. We were showered with gifts: letters from everyone, posters from our producers, cookies made with a picture of our playbill on them from Rachel, little cow keychains from Bruce Sabbath, chocolate lollipops from my parents, more ducks from Merete, metro cards from Jackie Hoffman, Schmackary's, flowers, alcohol, a violin brooch pin from Staś, and hats from Joel with our initials on them. Before the show began, the whole company got in a big circle on stage. Everyone made beautiful speeches, and then Joel walked around the circle to give each and every one of us a big hug. Then Ben Liebert, who is our Equity deputy, had all of the new Equity members come into the middle of the circle. Ben gifted us Equity swag, and everyone cheered for us as we ran around the circle, giving high fives all around. Then Ben read us Elia Kazan's poem, "The Actor's Vow." It was extremely moving to be surrounded by our *Fiddler* family on our opening night, while being initiated into the Actor's Equity Association with these beautiful words:

"I will take my rightful place on stage, and I will be myself.

I am not a cosmic orphan.

I have no reason to be timid. I will respond as I feel; awkwardly, vulgarly,

but respond.

I will have my throat open, I will have my heart open, I will be vulnerable.

I may have anything or everything the world has to offer, but the thing I need most, and want most,
is to be myself.

I will admit rejection, admit pain,

admit frustration, admit even pettiness, admit shame, admit outrage,

admit anything and everything that happens to me.

The best and most human parts of me are those I have inhabited

and hidden from the world. I will work on it.

I will raise my voice. I will be heard."

We cried happy tears, and then went back to our dressing rooms to get ready for opening night. We tightly squeezed each other's hands backstage before stomping on for "Tradition," and were greeted by the audience with the most enthusiastic entrance applause. It felt like a big welcome into our new home at Stage 42. I watched most of the show from the wings out of pure excitement. There was no milk jug in the wings for Rachel and me to sit on during "Do You Love Me," so I shifted a couple of stacked chairs for us to watch from before the number started, which became our new spot. In the fleeting moments of silence, I looked around at the beautiful theatre, and the high ceiling, and thought: *I am so happy to be here. I am so lucky to be here.* At the curtain call, the five daughters gave flowers to our fearless directors and lead actors. Joel made a wonderful, tear-jerking speech, and then the entire cast surrounded him in a big group hug.

We ran back to the dressing rooms, bouncing with excitement, and got into our opening night gowns. Everyone threw on extra makeup and touched up their hairstyles, chattering joyously about our opening night. Our opening night party was at Sardi's: the famous Broadway hang-out and restaurant on 44th street, where the Tony Award was birthed, and hundreds of caricatures of famous actors adorn the walls. I walked over to the party with Rachel, who put on her heels a block away like an expert. We hugged our families, took pictures on the red carpet, met celebrities, and celebrated the success of our Yiddish *Fiddler.* Jodi and I found Joel's caricature on the wall, and at the end of the night, Rachel and I snatched the "Joel Grey" signs from his reserved tables for keepsakes. I went home exhausted, and feeling like the luckiest girl in the world. It was a night that will live in my heart forever.

* * *

Jackie Hoffman

Role: Yente

I was brought up in an orthodox Jewish home, and I went to Yeshiva for nine years, so I had a really intense Jewish education. In my early teenage years, I was still super religious, and I belonged to an orthodox youth group. I went to Yeshiva High School, and then later switched to a public high school because I was going crazy with how many hours the Yeshiva High School was. In public school I got into acting — and that was it. I slowly started to drop the orthodox religion. It's always been in my gut and soul, but I stopped practicing all of the orthodox traditions for the rest of my life. I moved out, went to college, lived away from home with my roommates, and kind of just let it go. Now it seems like it's all flooding back to me. I'm looking at the word "Torah" every day, and I'm playing a really religious person; it's making me recall a time in my life when that was so important to me. The people in Anatevka function like their whole lives are so important, and it's

215

all based on that religious lifestyle. I used to be part of that world where everything was based on that. I've never done a show in Yiddish before, so that makes this a totally unique experience. I can't compare it to anything I've done in English. The connection to my family and my history from so long ago is a very cool thing for me.

I love coming out in the beginning of "Tradition." I want every show to start with the cast walking in a circle. It's very prideful; I rarely have pride in my real life, so it's great to come out with my chest lifted and the whole cast connected like that. It's like folk dancing, which is such an old form, but it feels timeless and very modern. It's a beautiful way of presenting our village. I also love selling the little boys to Shprintze and Beylke. Those are my favorite parts of the show.

Joel wanted to see me before the rehearsal process started. He just said "She's not—"

and I said, "I know what you mean; I'm not going to be the clown of the shtetl, don't worry about it." Two words were all I needed to hear. As always, Joel didn't want Yente to be too clownish. Like a good director does, he wanted me to be very true and honest with the moments. He said very poignant things about my scene at the end of the show — how she is really scared and doesn't know what is going to happen.

In my first scene in the show, I'm coming in very excited. I take any excuse to see my friend Golde, because I'm very lonely and for some reason, that I'm not aware of as Yente, everybody in the shtetl thinks that I'm a pain in the ass. I'm being a good businesswoman and giving this great news that I sealed the deal and got the richest man in town for her daughter. In my last scene, I am kind of desperate. Everything is lost; everything I worked so hard to build up is over. I'm really scared and I don't know what's going to happen. Both scenes have the same opening line, which I love: "Golde, I couldn't wait to see you; I have extraordinary news." It's a bookend sort of thing, and it's very effective. Towards the beginning of the run downtown, our Motl, played by Ben Liebert, missed his entrance in my first scene with Golde, played by Jennifer Babiak. We were left totally baking onstage and hadn't yet reached a point in which we could improvise in Yiddish. There was a long silence, and then I tried to think of anything I knew in Yiddish that I could say in that moment. I repeated a line that I have in the show and asked, "Where are your daughters?"

Then Jen replied, "Eh… daughters… outside!" It was tragically hilarious. At the time it was terrifying, but now that I've survived it, I consider it a funny mishap.

Working with Jennifer Babiak is the best. Jen is very "Jen-erous." She is a truly generous actress. She always gives a hundred percent. Whenever I want to check out and have no concentration, which happens all the time, I always look to Jen. She is constantly focused, professional, and at the highest emotional state. Since all of our scenes are together, she really helps me get into it a lot. It's always a challenge to keep the show fresh: like it's my first time doing it even when it's really my thousandth time. I have to remember that the audience is seeing it for the first time, aside from our super- fans. With the Yiddish it's important to always know what I'm saying and try to match each word with its meaning. Every word has a meaning — I don't always know what it is, but I have to act like I know exactly what I'm saying. It's also a technically challenging language. Today I spoke a wrong syllable on one word — I still make mistakes. Then Mikhl, a native Yiddish speaker in our cast, will speak in Yiddish and I will think, *Uh, we're not speaking the same thing. Mikhl is on a different level than everybody else.*

It's such a great cast to work with. There are no "celebrities" and it creates a whole different vibe than when you're on Broadway with some celebrity-status people. It's really loose, and everyone is so great. Bruce, our Leyzer-Volf, who is rich in real life too, has a house with a pool and graciously invited us over for a pool party last summer. I guess we got punished for swimming on Shabbos, because it was violently raining. It was a pool party, so we all swam anyway, because that's our cast. It was so fun. His wife, Karen, was like a hero and leant me a pair of socks when mine got soaking wet. I tried to give them back after I washed them, but Bruce insisted I keep them. That's the ultimate kindness — someone giving you a dry pair of socks. The day we recorded the cast album was my birthday. I had shot a television show that morning, and was running on barely any sleep, so I was in a different state of consciousness when I got to the recording. It was a strange and happy day; I love working on my birthday and it was so great spending the day with the cast. Adam Shapiro made me a beautiful "Hello Kitty" birthday cake, which was very fun. Backstage at the theatre, in my dressing room are three crazy dark broads: Rachel Zatcoff, Jennifer Babiak, and me. Jen is surprisingly funny. We get visitors, we have fun, we have ridiculous inside jokes, and when things are really getting to us, we all pass out on the floor. It's a good thing we have carpet.

* * *

Jennifer Babiak

Role: Golde

Playing Bobe Tsaytl was a great initiation into the Yiddish *Fiddler* world. I had never spoken Yiddish before, so it was really exciting to learn the part and get to dip my toes into the show in that way. In my career I've mostly played ingénues, so it was so much fun playing a character role. I remember having a conversation with Kayleen Seidl about understudying, because she was covering the three eldest daughters while I was covering Golde. Kayleen had all of her understudy roles memorized by the first week of rehearsal. I thought, *I guess I'd better get cracking on this understudy thing.* I'm glad I started working on it because I soon after had a coaching with Motl Didner and Zalmen Mlotek to work on the Golde material. Later that day I got a call from my agent saying that they wanted me to take over the role of Golde. I was really nervous, and wasn't even sure if I could do it. It would be my first time playing a mom, and it seemed very challenging in a lot of other ways as well. I woke up the next morning and thought: *Okay, I can do this.* I started coming home from rehearsal every night and just drilling the Golde material. In the beginning I kept thinking I was never going to "get" it, as far as the Yiddish. Then one day, it just clicked. I didn't have much rehearsal before my first day as Golde, so I had to do a lot of work on my own. I had two rapid-fire rehearsals with Joel Grey, and then suddenly I was performing the role with everyone live. I felt like the first week as Golde I was finding her voice. Golde is very earthy and grounded, and that's reflected in her speaking voice. My voice usually lives in "soprano-land," so it was fun finding where her voice sits in me. I see Golde as a motherly figure for the shtetl; she truly cares for everybody. She has eyes and ears in the back of her head in her own household, and also in the entire community. I picture her as the "Stretch Armstrong" of the shtetl — always looking out for everyone. I love this role so much. Even after a year of playing her, I'm constantly learning new things about Golde, and finding new moments in the show. It has just been a dream.

One of my favorite new moments that I've discovered is in "Sunrise Sunset." After the moms walk Tsaytl to Motl, I take a little walk to my spot: in that walk I get to look at the faces of all five of the daughters. I take a moment to think about the time passing, and when I look at them, I picture each one of them as they were when they were babies. I follow all of the girls' Instagram accounts, so I've seen many baby photos of them. I really picture those little faces in my mind when I'm singing about how just yesterday Tsaytl was playing in the yard. That moment of family nostalgia is very magical.

I've always liked the music in *Fiddler*, but I never realized how beautiful it really is until I got to sing it. It is so soulful and timeless, and I love getting to sing it every night. One of my favorite songs is "Do You Love Me." "Do You Love Me" has always been

portrayed as a comedic number, where Tevye and Golde play polar opposites. In our production, Tevye and Golde actually come together in that scene. Tevye has followed these love stories throughout the show, starting with Tsaytl and Motl, and Golde is finally catching up with him. "Do You Love Me" is this perfect scene where Tevye and Golde start out in completely different places and then somehow end up on the same page. They travel back to the beginning of their relationship together to get to that point of understanding. I think it is a perfect scene in a perfect musical. Joel Grey's staging of it is so simple and pure — even just Tevye putting his hand on Golde's shoulder is meaningful. It's made up of all these tiny little moments. Getting to work with Steven is unbelievable; we have so much fun onstage and offstage, and I love constantly finding new things within our scenes together. He is the most giving and present actor I have ever worked with.

When I found out that they wanted Steven and me to sing "Do You Love Me" at the Drama Desk Awards, my jaw dropped. The day of the awards, we had an early sound check at Town Hall, and then a matinee of *Fiddler.* I had an hour to get ready after *Fiddler,* so all of the girls came into my dressing room to help me. We played music, Rachel Zatcoff did my hair and makeup, and I borrowed a dress from Stephanie Lynne Mason. Rose Labarre, from our wardrobe team, highlighted me and sprayed me with things. It was so fun, and it was a beautiful time for us all to be together. Then my husband picked me up and we went to the red carpet. We took pictures, and I did some interviews. It was thrilling to be a part of the theatre community in that way: with everyone celebrating Broadway and Off-Broadway shows as peers on the red carpet. People were giving so much love to our show, and it was an amazing vibe all around. We sat in the audience for the awards, until they took Steven and me backstage before our performance.

The crowd went nuts after our performance. To do our number in Yiddish at the Drama Desk Awards and have everyone cheering like that was incredible. When we got back to our seats, they were announcing the winner for "Best Musical Revival." Being in that audience, right behind Joel Grey when they announced that *Fiddler* won the Drama Desk Award for best musical revival was unforgettable. We were all screaming and going crazy with joy. It was a beautiful night to celebrate theatre.

I will always remember our pre-rehearsal Yiddish coaching with Zalmen. We all gathered on the stage, and Zalmen told us to just pick a vocal part and try singing "Tradition." Steven started his monologue and then everyone sang together for the first time. I was blown away; it was so beautiful and powerful, and in that moment, I knew that this was going to be something special. I imagine that is what it's like when our audiences hear "Tradition" for the first time too.

The most challenging part of this process was the week of rehearsal leading up to the transfer to Stage 42. It was a really intense week, and trying to get the changes that Joel wanted from us in the new space was scary and difficult. I had all of these thoughts in my head, like: *can I do this? Is this going to work?* At the end of the day, Joel Grey was always right. Taking the leap and going there was scary, but we were all there to support each other through the challenges. In the end it was awesome and so worth it. I think Joel Grey was meant to direct *Fiddler*. He really understands these characters, and I've loved watching him work with everyone because everything he says is just golden.

We have really all found this lifelong family, which to me is the most beautiful part of this experience. It's been such an awesome journey working with Jackie Hoffman, too. We shared a dressing room at the theatre downtown, so I really got to know her on a personal level. We became very close friends, which helped form a relationship with Yente and Golde that I hadn't seen in productions before. Yente and Golde have a strong friendship, and I think that shines through in our interpretation. Jackie and I are really there for each other every night, on and off stage. I feel very safe onstage with both Steven and Jackie as my main scene partners. We are living, breathing actors up there, and finding the moments that we've found together over the process has been so cool. Everyone in the cast cares about each other so much; this shtetl is a real family. From the moment Steven starts the show, we are all in it together for the incredible, three-hour journey. Every single person put so much hard work into learning this language, these characters, this culture, and this show, without having any idea what would come out of it. We had no clue how it would be received, but now it has been one amazing thing after the next. We have all just been appreciating everything and living in the moment — without ever really knowing where this journey is taking us. It's a once in a lifetime experience, and it's so special to me.

Part Thirteen
Bashert

Sammy

Role: Beylke

In March, 2019, we started collecting money for the Broadway Cares Easter Bonnet Competition. The Easter Bonnet Competition involved a month of fundraising for Broadway Cares, followed by a performance with an original skit and bonnet to represent our show. We made speeches and collected money in red buckets after every show, and we rehearsed our skit, that Ben Liebert, Adam Shapiro, and Mikhl Yashinsky created, at the theatre between shows. The skit was called "Better in Yiddish," and was a medley of Yiddish versions of famous musicals. It ended with Joel singing "Give My Regards to Broadway" in Yiddish, from the musical *George M*, in which he originated the role of George M. Cohan in 1968. Sarah Dixie and Adam Shapiro created an amazing bonnet for us, made up of playbills with a Yiddish twist, like "Knish Me Kate," "Oyklahoma," and "The Phantom of the Matzah." I learned how to sign my name very fast, as playbills and posters from our show were constantly circulating the dressing room to be signed for selling to raise money. On the last day of fundraising, Joel came onstage and we auctioned off an experience for an audience member to be serenaded by him. We raised three thousand dollars that night: Joel sang his "When I was Eight Days Old" song to one audience member, "Willkommen" to the second, and "Give My Regards to Broadway" to the third. We all backed him up with "oompa-pas" on "Willkommen," thrilling over how amazing it was to be two feet away from him while he sang that song, which he originated as the Emcee in the musical *Cabaret* in 1966.

The Easter Bonnet Competition was two days long: we performed our skit twice on the Minskoff stage in front of two huge audiences, including the stars from the other Broadway and Off-Broadway musicals that were participating. In the morning of the first performance, we all went to the Minskoff theatre to have a quick tech rehearsal. We got to run the number twice through, with microphones and music, as they set the lighting cues for the performance. I was in awe at the hugeness of the stage at the Minskoff, and loved staring up at the giant set pieces from *The Lion King* that hung all around the backstage area. I couldn't believe that I was about to perform on my first Broadway stage; the enormity of the stage and the size of the audience was very daunting in itself. As I stood in the wings, waiting to run out on the stage to sing in the *Legally Blonde* portion of the song, I saw a little panel of the wall that had messages written all over it. As I got closer to it I realized that they were cute, encouraging notes that must have been written by *The Lion King* cast, or another company that had performed there before. It warmed my heart, and I thought about how lucky I was to be in such a beautiful, loving, community of artists. I started to try to think of what show was in the theatre before *The Lion King,* and it was then that I remembered that the Minskoff theatre was where one of my most cherished teachers and mentors, Randy Graff, had played Golde in *Fiddler on the Roof* on Broadway in 2004. The rush of realization felt like getting a big hug, and suddenly the theatre didn't feel so big and scary anymore. It felt like destiny-*bashert.*

Ben had directed the entire skit, and it turned out to be an absolute gem. The audience roared with laughter, and when we finished our performance, I heard the loudest applause I had ever heard in my life. On the second day of the competition, we did the exact same show for a different audience. At the end of all the performances on the second day, Bryan Cranston, Jeff Daniels, Glenda Jackson, and Kelli O'Hara presented awards to the winners of the best bonnet, best overall performance, and highest fundraiser. We won best overall performance, and highest Off-Broadway fundraising at $77,283. It was one of the most amazing experiences, and I was beyond elated to have shared it with my *Fiddler* mishpokhe.

Back at Stage 42, I got into the groove of being in a

long-running show for the first time; I had never been in a show that ran for more than a few performances before. Being in a long-running show gave us all the amazing opportunity to watch each other grow, onstage and offstage. I was constantly inspired by my castmates' originality and mutability: from Mikhl's marvelous speech in the wedding scene each night, to Raquel's spirited learning and usage of new Yiddish adlibs. I was gifted with the most generous scene partners- we constantly fed each other's performances and found new moments with each other on stage. We also were fed with energy by incredible audiences, talkbacks, and special events. Everyone came to the theatre ready to play, and eager to learn, so it never got stale. We kept a lot of the same traditions from downtown, and developed new ones as we went along. One day, Raquel had a lovely idea to write a letter to Danielle Allen and Emerson Glick, the Shprintze and Beylke from the *Fiddler on The Roof* Broadway North American Tour. The two of us wrote them a letter, and we became fast penpals. We wrote letters back and forth with them during shows, asking each other questions and relating over our roles, and it became a wonderful penpalship for all four of us. My favorite traditions, new and old, were writing letters to Danielle and Emerson, singing a phrase from *Into the Woods* with Jodi right before the show started, squeezing Ben Liebert's hand in "Tradition," dancing with Rachel Calter and Raquel before "Matchmaker," and watching "Do You Love

Me" with Rachel Zatcoff.

Between shows, we explored midtown lunch spots, got frozen yogurt from Pinkberry, sat in small gardens, discovered cute shops, and sometimes went to the park to play frisbee. Other times, we ate lunch in the upper lobby, where we could see the top of the marquee right in the window, and fell asleep on the bench there, listening to quiet music. On the days that I was especially tired, I took a blanket to the seats in the theatre and curled up under the arm rests for a nap. I always set an alarm on my phone for those naps, but was usually awoken by the sound of Jordan Porch testing the microphones on stage, which always gave me a moment to remember how lucky I was to be spending my time in a theatre. The best wakeup I had was after Jodi, Raquel, and I fell asleep on benches in the upper lobby after a matinee, and woke up to find out that Patti LuPone was coming to our evening show. I had never imagined myself actually getting to meet Patti LuPone in person, though I adore her to no end. She was gracious, passionate, hilarious, and generous with her time and kind words. We were constantly stunned by these amazing, star-struck moments, as highly esteemed celebrities often came to see our show. What was just as stunning were the moments when we gave autographs at our own stage door, and talked to audience members and fans at special events. What shocked me the most was that no matter how exciting and mind-blowing these experiences were, the magic and glamour of it all somehow just felt human and humbling at the end of the day. We were all just people, telling stories, creating things, and connecting in different ways.

On World Refugee Day, every seat at our theatre was underwritten by donors and we had a full house of refugees watching our show. It was an extremely moving connection and experience. Before the show started, we got to mingle with our guests in the upper lobby, and afterwards we had a talkback on the stage where the refugees shared their experiences and their own "*Fiddler* stories." It was so special to be telling the story of *Fiddler* to audience members who had endured similar atrocities to the characters we were portraying, and to then provide a safe environment where they could connect, share, and relate to each other. We heard some incredible and devastating stories that truly stuck with us. At the end of the talkback, a ten-year-old boy stood up from the audience and said, "I love this show. It reminds me of my home country of Venezuela. I have one message: never give up." His simple, important words, and all of their poignant stories, moved us to tears, and reminded us why we were telling the story of *Fiddler* eight times a week.

On May 11th, 2019, we had our one hundredth show of *Fiddler on the Roof in Yiddish* at Stage 42. Jodi and I went back and forth naming one hundred things we love about being in *Fiddler* on the subway ride over to the theatre. When we got ready for the show, everyone in the girls' dressing room went around and shared their favorite memories. There were so many incredible memories to choose from that it was actually hard to name just one. I put a jar and a stack of paper on the table in the green room, and we filled it with things we love about each other during the next couple of days. The jar was quickly stuffed with anonymous compliments and endearments for everyone in the company, and I took it home and turned it into a big poster for our hallway. One hundred shows had flown by so quickly that I couldn't even believe it had happened. After our hundredth show, we had a celebratory cake and a party in the upper lobby. At that party, our producers, Hal Luftig and Jana Robbins, announced that we would be extending until January 2020, and that we weren't stopping there. I couldn't believe my ears. We all cheered, cried, and threw ourselves into each other's arms. Our beautiful little show, which was supposed to run for only six weeks, was going to run for eighteen months. It was a "miracle of miracles."

* * *

Ben Liebert

Role: Motl

I thought that I was coming into this rehearsal process fully "getting" my character. What I was really coming in with was my old bag of tricks, which have worked many and oft. I usually get hired because I walk in with my skill set and use those things in the show. Joel was not having that, which was really fortunate in the long run. After the initial read-through I thought, *man, I crushed it. He's a wacky, neurotic guy. Now, what bits can I find?* I was getting laughs in a language nobody understood, and I felt like I just *got* it. Joel kept telling me to make him simpler, more honest, and more pure. There was one chat we had after rehearsal that I will always remember, after Rachel Zatcoff and I ran the pre-Sabbath scene. Joel said, "Great! Rachel, you can go." Then he sat me down and said, "I know what you're doing. I get it. I've been there. You're trying a million things and seeing what works. It's seeming a little... schticky." It really killed me to hear him say that; partly because *Joel Grey* was telling me what I was doing wasn't working, and partly because I really try to come at jokes from an honest place. It was a gut-punch, but I immediately also felt lucky that I had a director who was willing to say that to me. So many won't, or they won't be specific in what the problem is like that. I was really appreciative of his honesty.

I spent the next couple of days sitting in my backyard, writing down a bunch of words and figuring out what makes someone simple, honest, and pure. What I found is that Motl is not introspective — he doesn't think in that way. He's a weirdo who just shows up and has no idea he is being weird. I washed out all the old choices I had ever made, and came in as that person. Joel was really happy. From there, the humor started to come back. I remember Rachel and I talked about it too — she was always ready to roll with what I was trying out. I've learned so much about my character throughout this run that I actually want all of my friends who came and saw the show downtown to come back. I feel like I'm a lot better now. It's interesting to consider whether or not it's actually that different. I've been in shows that only run for three weeks, and seeing where I'm at now, I feel like I knew absolutely nothing three weeks into the run. I think it's just the nature of what we do, that I'm still discovering things this far into it. At this point in the run, you are either still inquisitive and find new things, or you become stale and start going through the motions. I've found a lot of new moments that I love. When Steven is yelling at me in the "Rebuttal" and asking who the match I have for Tsaytl is and I finally say, "It's me," I make this strange noise and then chew on my hand. It just came about weirdly and naturally, and I dig it. That whole scene with Steven is amazing. It's so structured but so organic every night. It's been a pleasure and a challenge to play; sometimes we will have an amazing moment, and sometimes I will try something that ends up not feeling completely right. I don't think it'll ever be set in stone.

Working with Rachel Zatcoff is awesome. Normally, in the jobs I've done, I play a funny sidekick, so I have rarely had a scene partner like that. I'm really thankful, because it could've been ugly. We work so well together; we listen to each other, and we enjoy each other's presence offstage. It's never a competition to us — we know what our jobs are in the play, and what roles our characters have in the storytelling. We really are a team, and I'm so thankful that I get to work with her. It's never about either one of us. It's a weird thing in "Miracle of Miracles" when she has to sit there and watch me sing, but it's really about the two of us, and it was always important for me that we were working on it together. "Miracle of Miracles" is a duet. In a way I wish she didn't have to just sit there, because there is so much give and take between the two of us as I'm figuring out all of these things in the song. Sometimes I feel like I'm a pinball bouncing around a stationary object; in reality, she is doing so much in that number — even my parents have said it. There is so much to be found in it when it is a duet: there are times to make her laugh, connect with her, thank her, go off and figure something out on my own, and check back in with her. Motl doesn't really do well on his own. The fact that he has her there is really the reason he sings.

I love the new lyrics for "Miracle of Miracles."

When I first got them, I was grumpy and offended. I didn't understand why we used the old lyrics downtown for six months if they were not right. The lyric changes are actually easier to sing, though, because the vowels are more helpful. There's also more variety in the lyrics, which allows for more discovery. Since we went back to the original lyrics that Sheldon Harnick wrote, the arc of the song makes more sense too. The story of Daniel in the Lion's Den, used in the original lyrics, is a much better analogy to what Motl is going through than the story of Moses and the Stone, the lyrics from the Shraga Friedman translation. It was terrifying to get completely new lyrics, but also it was an exciting challenge that helped me find new moments. In restaging the number for the transfer uptown, my excitement, enthusiasm, and connection with Rachel has gotten a little bit more honest, and also a little bit bigger. It was a win-win all over the place.

One of my favorite memories was in our first preview when the audience laughed at the "Sunrise, Sunset" lyric: "When did he get to be so tall?" It was ironic because I am so short. None of us had thought of it: we had just been worried about getting the Yiddish right, and didn't think of the fact that it worked on multiple levels. Another favorite is when Frank Oz came to see our show — I recognized him right away and lost my mind. You don't realize until you meet certain people how formative they were in your life. I was able to stand there with him, his son, Steven, and

Bruce, and chat for fifteen minutes. If it was any other person, they would have been swamped, and I wouldn't have been able to express what I felt, so that was really special.

I really try to stop and smell the roses with this. Working at home on a show that people really like is incredible. I've never been in something like this. I've been in a Broadway show, but the Broadway show was already running — it was a machine. People would appreciate it, but it was what it was. I've been in regional shows that people loved and were really fun, but they had to close when they were scheduled to close so that the next thing could open. I think we are really fortunate. Since I'm a pragmatist I'm kind of waiting for the shoe to drop and for this to just feel like a job. It might happen, and it might come in waves for all of us — but hopefully it won't. Hopefully this family, as dysfunctional as we are, won't break up.

* * *

Rachel Zatcoff

Role: Tsaytl

I was paired with four different 'Motls' during the callbacks; working with Ben Liebert was the best. I distinctly remember doing the callback with Ben, thinking it felt really good, and actually skipping out of the audition room together in joy. It was kind of adorable. Working with Ben is incredible; I've felt really comfortable with him from day one. We always would talk privately after rehearsal with Joel, and communicate about how we were feeling and what we were thinking in regards to our characters and the scene work. Our first scene has evolved so much from the beginning of the run: I now really feel like I'm in a scene with my childhood "bestie." On top of that, there is a major element of the exciting, forbidden love. The stakes feel much higher than they were when we first started rehearsing the scene, but at the same time it feels more comfortable. I love Ben. We are constantly telling each other how grateful we are that the other person is the other person. Doing "Miracle of Miracles" with him is the best thing ever; we are expressing our gratitude through our eyes in every moment of that whole entire scene. It feels like we are looking at each other during the song and both saying with our eyes: "I love you, and I'm so grateful for this moment every single day."

Having four new little sisters onstage and offstage is wild. I don't have any real- life sisters, but I feel like the five of us operate as real sisters. As much as we annoy each other sometimes offstage, I have a very deep fondness of all four of them on a very sisterly level. I feel like we have all learned each other's quirks, differences, similarities, and nerves. The good and the bad that we have witnessed in each other brings itself into the show in a really close, cozy, irritated way. It's all of the things I would imagine you would feel with a sister. Despite all of our differences, I would hurt someone for literally all four of them. As the oldest, I feel that motherly nature as well where I feel very protective over all of them. At the same time, I can roll my eyes at one of them about the other one, without the other one seeing it. It's the greatest thing. One of my favorite things that I do with Stephanie and Rosie is a little tradition we have right before we go onstage for "Matchmaker." One of us could be having a really bad day, one of us could be having the best day ever, or one of us could barely be talking to the other, and right before "Matchmaker" the three of us get into a little huddle and pick a dirty word or phrase for the scene. It's become this sisterly tradition — we smack each other and jump around and then they *push* me onto the stage. Honestly, the dirty word has nothing to do with anything but it's just this fun, weird thing we do that I think real-life sisters would do. There's something playful about it that helps jumpstart the scene, and I love it.

Working on my scene with Tevye before the first "Rebuttal" was very frustrating in the beginning. I came into the early rehearsal process thinking that I knew what the scene was all about, when really I didn't. Joel was extremely hard on me, and the whole thing was so frustrating to me that every time I saw the scene listed on the rehearsal schedule, I would have a panic attack before heading into the room. I have very vivid memories of one day when we were rehearsing the scene in the big banquet room upstairs. Joel was really on my case, saying, "You're kvetching! You're kvetching! Stop kvetching! She's not a kvetch! She's not crying — she's strong!" It was against everything that I thought the scene was. What I now realize is that Joel just didn't want to allow me to go to that emotional place yet, because I wasn't ready to go there at the time. I thought that I was, but I really wasn't because I hadn't gone through all of the other things to actually get there. I remember sitting on the bench and deliberately taking deep breaths: thinking that I was going to lose it, but being determined not to. Steven Skybell then started taking deep breaths with me while sitting beside me on the bench, which I will never forget. At the end of that rehearsal, I was walking out of the room and Joel turned around in his seat and said, "I love you, Rachel Zatcoff. I love you." After two hours of having him grill me in the scene, I was thinking, *you love me? You're kinda torturing me! What does that mean?*

The scene was that way for a while downtown — me being strong, like a wall, and not crying. Towards the end of the run downtown, Joel came up to me backstage during a performance and said, "Maybe she cries." I just looked at him. Then I said, "What?"

He replied, "Maybe she cries a little bit. When she says she would be unhappy. Maybe just a little bit, if it comes." After that, I would allow myself to get a little more emotional at that part of the scene. Then we started rehearsing for the uptown transfer and Joel said, "In this scene, she is sobbing the whole time." Now that is where we are with it, but I still feel like I have every single part of what it was downtown in the scene. It's so interesting — she is feeling all of the things. I feel like he needed me to go through all of those things in order to give me permission to really be there, sobbing. I'm not striving for consistency or perfection — I'm just trying to be present. Everything feels freer from that. It really feels like this process, and working with this group, is making us all better actors. Everybody is so "dropped in" most of the time, and that is a true blessing. I have given myself more freedom, and as long as I'm locked into my intention and my scene partner's eyeballs, everything is going to be fine.

When I think of what my memories will be of this experience, I think of the rehearsal process. The rehearsals were so special, unique, and focused. Another one of my favorite memories was recently uptown, when Joel showed up backstage at our performance, as he often does. He came into my shared dressing room with Jackie Hoffman and Jennifer Babiak, and started singing songs from *Stop the World I Want to Get Off.* I was thinking, *this is crazy. I am in a theatre that I used to drive by every time I entered the city as a child, coming out of the Lincoln tunnel. Now I'm here performing in this show, and Joel Grey is in my dressing room singing these songs that he used to sing on stage. This is a moment.* I also have a very fond memory of sitting next to Joel during a rehearsal downtown of "The Dream." Everyone but me was rehearsing "The Dream," and he was enjoying a bagel with lox and cream cheese next to me. He turned to me and said, "Isn't this show so good? Aren't you glad you're not in this number?" He was just loving his little bagel and it was the cutest thing ever. I said, "Yes, Joel. It's so good and I'm so glad I'm not in this number." Every single part of this experience is one giant beautiful memory for me that feels like a once-in-a-lifetime thing.

The most amazing part of this experience is this group of people. It's such a troop of different folks — all different ages, experiences, and backgrounds. I have never worked with a group of people like this where I feel like every single person wants to be here. Not only do they want to be here — they're overflowing with joy and gratitude to be here, and that's really special. It *should* be why everyone wants to do this. It feels like everyone here is in this business because they enjoy the work and are open to learning and excited to tell this story. Sure, we all have our days and our moments, but the second "Tradition" starts and everyone starts stomping their feet — we are all right there, together. Joel came to see a performance last week when there were a lot of understudies on and he said to me, "Everyone is just supporting each other. Everyone just supports each other and lifts each other up!" That's what it is. Also, watching Steven play a role that he was born to play is incredible: that marriage of role and human only comes along once in a blue moon. He is so lucky, and we are so lucky to witness it. No matter who is out, and no matter who is having a bad day — our show is still our show. We all have been told from day one how special this is. Mandy Patinkin came to our show and said, "Someday you'll know how special this is." When I think about that, I think the truth with us is that we all know right now, in the moment, how special this is. That's what makes it even more special: we don't need to wait ten years to listen to a recording in a car. We know it now — you can feel it radiating off of our bodies onstage and offstage. It's so special and beautiful, and it's the most meaningful thing I've ever done. It may be the most meaningful thing I ever do, and that's okay. If this is the most meaningful and special thing I ever do, that would really be okay.

* * *

Steven Skybell

Role: Tevye

The challenge of the Yiddish was really interesting and wonderful. Working on this brought it all back to acting 101, because knowing what you are saying isn't enough; you have to also know what the other person is saying too. Often, we can forget that because they're speaking English, but having to stop and say, "wait, I don't really know exactly what my scene partner is saying to me," and figuring it out adds a whole new element. Having to know everyone's lines was actually very helpful. I had to crack open the script more than I would for any classic Broadway piece. It was a great opportunity to explore the script in a deeper way than if it had been only in English. People have said to me, "You've created such a different Tevye," but I don't really feel that way. I don't feel like I've intentionally tried to create anything other than what is on the page. I do think the Yiddish helps it feel new. Another aspect of it is that there aren't a lot of roles that I have known, wanted to do, and done for the majority of my life. That's actually crazy cool, because I have an opinion about every moment in the show, even the moments I'm not in. It's stuff I know from having seen it and performed in it, and just having thought about it. With this production it often felt like I knew exactly what to do in most moments, and I don't even know where I came up with it, because it's kind of from the deep recesses.

I had several Yiddish coachings with Motl Didner before we started rehearsal, and I remember just stopping and turning to Motl and saying, "Wait, Tevye is still talking? He has not left the stage?" It's a very large part, and I didn't quite know that going into it. I've done some large Shakespearean roles, and it's like that in the sense that you really have to use your energy in a way that will work for three hours. It's been a challenge to want to give my all, but also not blow my voice out during every performance. I've had to learn what I can do, and how I can do it smartly, while not feeling like I'm sailing through it. That's always been a big thing of mine — I want it to feel and sound real. That sometimes has to come at a vocal cost for me. Playing Tevye when I was seventeen and twenty-one were actually very meaningful experiences for me, but they were both only for a few performances. In comparison to playing Tevye every day for over a year now, it's amazing to have survived the role so far. It has been a fun challenge, but it definitely takes a lot out of me. I think all actors want to be given those opportunities to really push themselves. There is a lot that I can't do in my life because I have to do the show. I don't want to do anything that would tire me or maybe hurt me, and for now that's fine.

I heard in an interview that Joel Grey once thought he was going to play Tevye one day, so the thing about him is that he has lots of ideas about who Tevye is. I feel like I know this musical and it comes from a deep place, but there were many times in rehearsal where Joel would say something and I would stop in my tracks and think, *hmmm!* I never had a moment of thinking he was wrong; I always wanted to do what he suggested. Often it was different than what my instincts would have led me to, and I love that. More often than not it was about taking out a sort of bombast, bluster, or buffoonery of Tevye. He was always encouraging me to be true, simple, and real. That's really what every actor wants to do, so to be given that sort of direction was wonderful. I always like that — being given the allowance to calm down and make it simpler.

I've already said Joel Grey is a fantastic director, but one favorite story I have is from working on "The Dream" with him. Whenever we were working on it, he would give me these directions like, "I don't believe you're really sleeping." I was so confused, and then I finally said, "Tevye didn't really have this dream, right, Joel?" Joel said, "No, he had this dream. This is a dream he had." I said, "I've always thought that Tevye is making up this dream."

He said, "I'll be right back," and went to the other room to confer with Zalmen Mlotek. When he came back, he said I was right to say that Tevye is making up the dream. That's the only thing that Joel was ever a little unclear of. In the original script, it may have been unclear, but in the way we do it, I am definitely making it up.

I love working with Jennifer Babiak, who plays Golde. I don't know how she considers herself as an actor or performer, but I know she has probably done mostly musical theatre in the past. That possibly being the case, I have seen her become this acting monster on the stage. When we came uptown for the transfer, Joel pushed her hard. He pushed us all, but he specifically still had some strong, clear ideas of what he thought Golde needed to be. He pushed her to go harder and deeper, and she never buckled under that kind of pressure. As far as I can tell, she just took what he said and is flying with it now. In the scene where she runs on stage to tell me that Khave has gotten married, my work is so easy. Every night she comes in heartbroken, and it is so beautiful, deep, and sad. She is the one that has to come on with all of that stuff, and she just serves it up to me. That is a joy, because I don't have to manufacture anything, I just have to respond to what she is truly giving me.

Doing this show in Yiddish has made it very special. I jokingly say that when I got cast in this show I rolled my eyes and thought, *well, I'm finally playing Tevye at the right age, but now it's in Yiddish.* I never thought it would be so embraced by the public at large. I love doing it in Yiddish. It's also terrible to say, but this classic Broadway musical from the '60s is so timely right now. It's crazy, but it feels wonderful to put our energy and intent into this story and let it be something that can help with the conversation at large now. I've always loved this musical, but I love it even more now. I love doing it. The people are fantastic. Joel has said to us so many times that our company is unique in that respect. Everyone is giving their all, and everyone is so loving and supportive of each other.

* * *

Joel Grey

Director

We expected it to be a very difficult show to cast in that twenty-eight people needed to sing well, act well, and sound as if they were totally at home with the Yiddish language. HA! Turns out that there was a tremendous interest in this strange and wonderful project, and we had a couple thousand responses to auditioning. There were many, many very good people who had, in fact, worked on their own in order to audition something in Yiddish. In certain circumstances, they needed to dance very demanding Jerome Robbins choreography as re-conceived by Staś Kmieć. Casting Tevye was, truth to tell, the most crucial casting we made. There were a number of good Tevyes that auditioned, but when Steven Skybell came in and sang "If I Were a Rich Man" in perfect Yiddish and perfect intention, it was a revelation. Once we settled on Steven as our Tevye, I knew our biggest obstacle was completed. As with any new project without the complexity of another language, the time frame made the need to make decisions quickly. Thank God, they turned out to be the right decisions.

There were some people, as always, who took more time to find their way, and there's always that moment where the director wonders whether he's made a mistake. Everybody has their own way of working:

247

some slow, and some very quick. Sometimes you're not sure whether the actor was in fact the wrong choice or just not up to the challenge. There were all those questions up until days before our first preview. Luckily for me, everybody came through with flying colors. But I had my moments. Yikes! I think the second act situation with Khave and Fyedke and Tevye and Golde was very challenging and risky. It turns out the actors were up to the challenge.

Staś and I worked before we started production with a mini version of the set with mini chairs and mini tables, trying to figure out and imagine the show. During all of this, we relied on the stage management team, Kat West, Rachel Calter, and Lindsay Jones, and my wonderful assistant Max Sterling among others to guide and keep us on track. Our designer team, including Beowulf Boritt, Ann Hould-Ward, Peter Kaczorowski, Dan Moses Schreier, Tom Watson, and Addison Heeren, worked against all odds to make it beautiful. Of course, Zalmen's dream-show turned out to be exactly that. His vision and musical acuity were superb. We were all so enormously aided by Motl Didner and Sabina Brukner. Of great assistance were Sean Patrick and Britni Serrano as well.

I relate to just about everything in this musical. It is in many ways the story of all of our lives. Looking for a home. Not finding it. Finding it again. And ultimately, handling the joys and tragedies of life itself under fire. Everything about this production is special. Absolutely everything. I believe we were touched by some kind of angel in that it was so unlikely a success and yet this motley, magnificent group of us, out of love, rose to the occasion.

Epilogue
Mit Libe

Sammy

Role: Beylke

Recently the whole cast performed in a gala that was honoring Joel Grey down at the National Yiddish Theatre Folksbiene. We went down to the theatre in Battery Park on a Friday morning to rehearse before our evening performance of *Fiddler* back at Stage 42. A lot of us were early, so we ventured to the field of grass beside the theatre, and Evan took out a big picnic blanket for us to all lay on. We lay in the grass, listening to music and looking at the clouds, in the same spot that we lay in a year before, on Evan's last day downtown. When we went inside the museum, everything seemed different to me. I couldn't stop thinking about how small everything looked: the theatre, the seats, the lobby, the wings, the backstage crossover. Everything that had felt so huge and mysterious to me last summer suddenly seemed so simple and small. All of my fond memories came flooding back, feeling like the most precious dream.

As we were about to start the rehearsal, Zalmen

said, "Let's just pause here for a minute. I just want to take a second to acknowledge where we are right now, and that we are all here together. This is where we started." I thought about learning to roll my "r"s and how to put on a shmata, watching Joel eat cough drops, walking in circles while pumping my arms, sucking my thumb, screaming in an elevator with my show sisters, waiting in the wings to run on for the first scene, getting cut from numbers and eating emergency chocolates, and sitting on the milk jug backstage. All of the huge milestones and dreams that came true for me during this experience were surpassed in my mind by the little moments of love — *libe*.

When Rachel and I got released from rehearsal, we left the theatre together and ran into Joel sitting on a bench outside. He gave us each a big hug and said, "How wonderful is this? We are moving people. We get to move people all the time." We beamed at him, and I thought: *That is why we are here.* There is no place I would rather be.